D0577618

LOST CIVILIZATIONS

THE ANCIENT EGYPTIANS

Allison Lassieur

LUCENT BOOKS
P.O. BOX 289011
SAN DIEGO, CA 92198-9011

Other titles in the *Lost Civilizations* series include:

The Ancient Greeks
The Ancient Romans
Empires of Mesopotamia
The Mayans

On Cover: Ancient fragment depicting a banquet with dancers and musicians playing songs written above them.

Library of Congress Cataloging-in-Publication Data

Lassieur, Allison.
The ancient Egyptians / by Allison Lassieur.
p. cm. — (Lost civilizations)
Includes bibliographical references (p.) and index.
Summary: Discusses the history, daily life, social structure, art and religion, belief in the afterlife, and other aspects of ancient Egyptian civilization.
ISBN 1-56006-755-1 (lib. : alk. paper)
1. Egypt—Civilization—To 332 B.C.—Juvenile literature. [1. Egypt—Civilization—To 332 B.C.] I. Title. II. Lost civilizations (San Diego, Calif.)
DT61 .L36 2001
932'.01—dc21

00-008655

P.O. Box 289011, San Diego, CA 92198-9011
Printed in the U.S.A.

Contents

Foreword

"What marvel is this?" asked the noted eighteenth-century German poet and philosopher, Friedrich Schiller. "O earth . . . what is your lap sending forth? Is there life in the deeps as well? A race yet unknown hiding under the lava?" The "marvel" that excited Schiller was the discovery, in the early 1700s, of two entire ancient Roman cities buried beneath over sixty feet of hardened volcanic ash and lava near the modern city of Naples, on Italy's western coast. "Ancient Pompeii is found again!" Schiller joyfully exclaimed. "And the city of Hercules rises!"

People had known about the existence of long lost civilizations before Schiller's day, of course. Stonehenge, a circle of huge, very ancient stones had stood, silent and mysterious, on a plain in Britain as long as people could remember. And the ruins of temples and other structures erected by the ancient inhabitants of Egypt, Palestine, Greece, and Rome had for untold centuries sprawled in magnificent profusion throughout the Mediterranean world. But when, why, and how were these monuments built? And what were the exact histories and beliefs of the peoples who built them? A few scattered surviving ancient literary texts had provided some partial answers to some of these questions. But not until Pompeii and Herculaneum started to emerge from the ashes did the modern world begin to study and reconstruct lost civilizations in a systematic manner.

Even then, the process was at first slow and uncertain. Pompeii, a bustling, prosperous town of some twenty thousand inhabitants, and the smaller Herculaneum met their doom on August 24, A.D. 79 when the nearby volcano, Mt. Vesuvius, blew its top and literally erased them from the map. For nearly seventeen centuries, their contents, preserved in a massive cocoon of volcanic debris, rested undisturbed. Not until the early eighteenth century did people begin raising statues and other artifacts from the buried cities; and at first this was done in a haphazard, unscientific manner. The diggers, who were seeking art treasures to adorn their gardens and mansions, gave no thought to the historical value of the finds. The sad fact was that at the time no trained experts existed to dig up and study lost civilizations in a proper manner.

This unfortunate situation began to change in 1763. In that year, Johann J. Winckelmann, a German librarian fascinated by antiquities (the name then used for ancient artifacts), began to investigate Pompeii and Herculaneum. Although he made some mistakes and drew some wrong conclusions, Winckelmann laid the initial, crucial groundwork for a new science—archaeology (a term derived from two Greek words meaning "to talk about ancient things.") His book,

History of the Art of Antiquity, became a model for the first generation of archaeologists to follow in their efforts to understand other lost civilizations. "With unerring sensitivity," noted scholar C. W. Ceram explains, "Winckelmann groped toward original insights, and expressed them with such power of language that the cultured European world was carried away by a wave of enthusiasm for the antique ideal. This . . . was of prime importance in shaping the course of archaeology in the following century. It demonstrated means of understanding ancient cultures through their artifacts."

In the two centuries that followed, archaeologists, historians, and other scholars began to piece together the remains of lost civilizations around the world. The glory that was Greece, the grandeur that was Rome, the cradles of human civilization in Egypt's Nile valley and Mesopotamia's Tigris-Euphrates valley, the colorful royal court of ancient China's Han Dynasty, the mysterious stone cities of the Maya and Aztec in Central America—all of these and many more were revealed in fascinating, often startling, if sometimes incomplete detail by the romantic adventure of archaeological research. This work, which continues, is vital. "Digs are in progress all over the world," says Ceram. "For we need to understand the past five thousand years in order to master the next hundred years."

Each volume in the *Lost Civilizations* series examines the history, works, everyday life, and importance of ancient cultures. The archaeological discoveries and methods used to gather this knowledge are stressed throughout. Where possible, quotes by the ancients themselves, and also by later historians, archaeologists, and other experts support and enliven the text. Primary and secondary sources are carefully documented by footnotes and each volume supplies the reader with an extensive Works Consulted list. These and other research tools, including glossaries and time lines, afford the reader a thorough understanding of how a civilization that was long lost has once more seen the light of day and begun to reveal its secrets to its captivated modern descendants.

Introduction

Unlocking Egypt's Secrets

The Great Pyramid of Giza stands with two others at the edge of the desert. Today these pyramids are tourist attractions, crowded with people by day and flooded with golden lights by night. They symbolize a long-vanished civilization and represent a time when Egypt was the most powerful empire in the world.

The pyramids are not the only remnant of this ancient society, however. There is the Valley of the Kings, where pharaohs went to meet eternity and tomb robbers plundered dizzying amounts of gold and riches. In the cracked temples, massive statues still stare outward at the world just as they have done for thousands of years. Temple columns march in straight rows, and the calm Sphinx crouches at the base of the pyramids. Deep inside buried tombs, paintings and hieroglyphs show a world that lasted for more than three thousand years.

There is so much left of the ancient Egyptian civilization that it is hard to believe the culture lay shrouded in mystery for centuries. Even as warfare and invasion weakened ancient Egypt, writers and tourists from Greece and Rome came to the grand Egyptian cities and recorded the strange and wonderful things they saw there. But as Egypt came under foreign rule, people forgot how to read the Egyptian language, and the story of the civilization that once commanded the world was gone for good. For centuries, only tales of the once-great civilization would remain.

Eventually, Egypt came under Muslim rule, and few Europeans were allowed to visit. In the Middle Ages, sight-seeing knights on their way to battle in the holy lands floated up the Nile and glimpsed Egypt's mysterious wonders. But no one knew anything about the people or the civilization that had created such majesty.

When French commander Napoléon's troops invaded Egypt in 1798, they plundered vast amounts of Egyptian treasures and brought them back to France. In the years that followed, artists and tourists visited and sketched the strange temple ruins and bizarre statuary and sold their work to Europeans hungry for anything new and exotic.

During the 1800s, archaeologists and treasure hunters by the thousands invaded the once-silent Egyptian desert. Some came to study the culture, but others plundered ancient tombs for gold and valuable artifacts. Europeans embraced everything Egyptian and flocked to Egypt on grand vacation tours.

The Rosetta Stone

Even as Egyptian travel and artifacts became more accessible, the civilization's form of writing, hieroglyphs, tantalized scholars around the world. In 1799 one of Napoléon's soldiers found a strange stone fragment near Rosetta, Egypt. It was a black slab that had three groups of writing on it: hieroglyphs, ancient Greek, and an ancient form of Arabic. Scholars immediately realized that it was their strongest clue to breaking the code of the heiroglyphs, so

Serving as a symbol of ancient Egyptian civilization, the Great Pyramid of Giza (pictured) recalls the era when Egypt was the most powerful empire in the world.

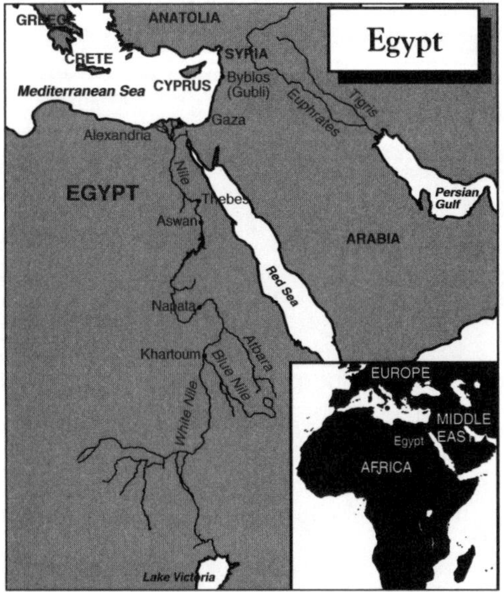

they made dozens of casts and copies of the writing on the Rosetta Stone. One of these copies made its way to the hands of a twelve-year-old French boy named Jean-François Champollion.

From that moment, Champollion's lifelong ambition was to be the first person to decipher the hieroglyphs. He prepared by studying ancient languages such as Coptic, Arabic, Hebrew, Latin, and Greek. Champollion struggled for years, and finally, in 1822, he broke the code of the hieroglyphs. The ancient civilization was revealed to the world at last.

And what a world it was. The ancient Egyptians had a knack for recording the mundane details of everyday life, from grocery lists to diaries and journals. Everyone, from pharaohs to peasants, came to life with their words. Almost overnight the civilization of the ancient Egyptians went from mysterious to understood.

Chapter One

Before the Egyptians

Ancient Egypt was the first, the largest, and the greatest early civilization in the world. During more than three thousand years of its history, Egypt dominated all other civilizations in every conceivable way—language, art, warfare, literature, economy, and culture. To those who lived at the time, Egypt was the world: powerful, unchanging, and eternal.

The ancient Egyptians who walked the sunlit streets of their glorious cities thought little of the earliest history of their land. If an ordinary Egyptian were asked about the beginnings of the Egyptian civilization, he might tell the story of Horus and Seth, two gods who battled over control of Egypt. Or he might tell about Egyptian kings and describe an offering he had recently made to such a ruler. If pressed, some Egyptians could probably explain that in the time before kings, spirits controlled Egypt. The Egyptians believed that their world had always existed as a powerful, vibrant culture.

However, there is much more to ancient Egypt than gods and spirits. In reality, there were two ancient Egypts, and both are distinct from one another. One was the Egypt of the pyramids, temples, and kings, which lasted from about 3100 B.C. to about 300 B.C. This is the civilization that most modern people know. The other was the Egypt before recorded history, when nomadic bands settled in villages and farmed along the banks of the Nile.

Differences Between Predynastic and Dynastic Egypt

The era known as the predynastic period lasted from about 5000 B.C. to about 3100 B.C. It is the time before kings ruled the land, and it is also the time before hieroglyphs, the written language of the ancient Egyptians. The time that followed is called dynastic, the period when kings unified and controlled Egypt. Everything that people today think of when they envision Egypt comes from the dynastic period.

The people of predynastic Egypt did not have a written language. They did, however, make attempts to record their lives with pictograms and other picture-based forms of writing. Their pictures were simple and showed common aspects of their lives. It is unclear when or how these crude pictures developed into hieroglyphs, for there are no artifacts or records showing a jump from pictures to language. However, by the beginning of the dynastic period, hieroglyphs were well developed.

Although the transition from predynastic to dynastic took hundreds of years, the people of predynastic Egypt were not idle. Their lives and innovations laid the foundation for everything that was to come after them. As historian Michael Hoffman so clearly explains,

> The Predynastic era was a critical time for the formation of later ancient Egyptian culture—a time during which the economic, political, and social underpinnings of pharaonic culture took on a distinctively Egyptian form. It is a period that witnessed the introduction and formative development of the mainstays of later historic ancient Egyptian society: effective farming and herding, metallurgy, pottery making, the shaping of hard stone by grinding, ceremonial architecture, elaborate burials, effective river-going sailing craft, long-distance trade, and stratified political and social systems.[1]

Little Evidence of Predynastic Egypt

The predynastic era stretches so far back in time that it is difficult to pinpoint its beginnings, although it is likely that nomads migrated to the area more than seven thousand years ago. Very little evidence exists about early predynastic Egypt, and archaeologists have had a difficult time reconstructing life during this period for a number of reasons. The greatest problem is, as Hoffman described, the lack of evidence. He says, "Egyptian prehistory suffers from the more fragmented and incomplete nature of its basic information—the archaeological remains."[2]

The earliest nomads moved from place to place, and archaeologists occasionally find small treasures: a flint tool here, a pottery shard there, to prove that someone had once passed by. But without other evidence, these tiny, tantalizing clues do little to unlock the

This engraving depicts agricultural methods in use in Egypt during the Predynastic era.

secrets of the people who made and used them.

It is not clear when the Nile valley was settled, but by around 5500 B.C. there is evidence that people were building villages and farming the land. These people made objects such as pottery, simple jewelry, clothing, and weapons. Most people stayed put for their entire lives. These farming communities thrived for hundreds of years.

This culture is also difficult to reconstruct because archaeologists themselves have destroyed the very things they need to study. During the nineteenth century, archaeologists scrambled to find gold and other precious artifacts. Few people were interested in pottery shards or bone fragments, and many archaeologists ignored or destroyed these objects. Thousands of clues to life in predynastic Egypt were destroyed, burned, thrown away, or allowed to fall into ruin.

Even when archaeologists did try to preserve the so-called less valuable Egyptian artifacts of prehistory, they were ill equipped to do so. Nineteenth-century archaeology was still in its infancy as a science, and archaeologists armed with shovels and picks inadvertently destroyed much evidence. The scientists did not know how to excavate a site because, in many cases, no one had done it before. As a result, some of the most valuable early artifacts were destroyed by the very scientists who had found them.

The grand Nile was also an enemy. Centuries of yearly flooding destroyed most of the remains of Egypt's earliest inhabitants, so today there is little left to find. The objects that are found, such as pottery fragments, are so rare it is almost impossible to use them to reconstruct the lives of predynastic people.

Another culprit is humanity itself. Egypt has been habitated for thousands of years, and this never-ending crush of people obliterated a vast amount of objects and structures that were made by early Egyptians. Ruins were torn down to make room for new buildings, lands that had once held large farming villages were plowed year after year, and cities were built upward on top of the remains of smaller towns.

Despite the lack of evidence, however, archaeologists have found enough to piece together a picture of life in predynastic Egypt. The emerging picture is of a culture laying the artistic, religious, and political foundations that would one day make Egypt the greatest civilization in the world.

The Nile: The Blood of Egyptian Culture

No Egyptian civilization could have survived without the Nile River. Egypt is a desert, and the Nile is one of the only sources of water. The earliest Egyptians clearly understood that the Nile was, literally, a source of life or death for them. Historian Adolph Erman is not exaggerating when he says,

> We now realize that [the Nile's] influence on Egyptian history and prehistory has been neither passive nor wholly benign. For instance, the annual inundations that are the backbone of Egypt's phenomenal fertility were . . . the cause of much public anxiety. If the inundations were too high, whole towns could be wiped out and thousands would perish in sudden deluges or later of starvation.[3]

The Nile shaped everything that the Egyptian culture was to become, including its religious

HERODOTUS AND THE MYSTERY OF THE NILE

The Nile has always played a vital role in Egyptian history. The ancient Egyptians, and foreign travelers alike, struggled to understand the mystical workings of the Nile. In the fifth century B.C., a Greek historian named Herodotus traveled throughout Egypt and recorded what he saw and heard. His book, *The Histories*, is one of the earliest written accounts of the ancient Egyptian civilization as seen by an outsider. The mysteries of the Nile especially intrigued Herodotus. He went to great lengths to discover the causes of the Nile's yearly floods. He sought out wise Egyptians who could answer his questions, and during his investigation, he heard three different theories. One idea suggested that winds prevented the Nile from flowing into the sea, which caused it to flood. A second theory suggested that the Nile moved in the same way as the ocean. The third theory, however, interested him the most.

Herodotus describes it in *The Histories*.

"The third theory, despite being the most plausible, is also the furthest from the truth. It claims the water of the Nile comes from melting snow, but this is just as nonsensical as the others. The Nile flows from Libya and through the middle of Ethiopia until it ends up in Egypt. How then, could it rise in snowy regions when its course takes it from the hottest places to places which are, by and large, cooler?"

Herodotus dismissed the third theory out of hand, insisting that it was too farfetched to be considered. Although he did not know it, the third theory was the closest to the truth—but it would take another two thousand years or so to discover it. In 1858 a British explorer named John Hanning Speke discovered the source of the Nile: Lake Victoria in Africa. Lake Victoria is in a mountainous region, and the seasonal rains in the area did indeed cause the yearly flooding far away in Egypt.

practices, its economy, and the very fabric of daily life. The river was so vital to the Egyptians that they created prayers and songs for it. This Egyptian prayer, for example, gives historians insight into the way that predynastic Egyptians viewed the life-giving power of the river. It reads, "Praise to thee, O Nile, that issues from the earth, and comes to nourish Egypt. . . . That waters the meadows he that [the god] Re [or Ra] created to nourish all cattle. That gives drink to the desert places, which are far from water, it is his dew that falls from heaven."[4]

Two Lands Along the Nile

The Nile shaped Egypt in different ways, creating two distinct predynastic groups. In the regions to the south, the river created a grand valley. This valley of Upper Egypt was filled with swamps, marshlands, and an abundance of water creatures and fish. The people who emerged in this area relied on hunting and gathering, creating a restless, nomadic culture that focused on possession and conquest of land.

As the Nile flowed north, it created a fertile triangular area at the Mediterranean Sea. The area, known as Lower Egypt, was perfect for growing crops of wheat and barley. The people who settled in this area built villages and grew crops, creating stable societies that relied on trade, government, and spiritual beliefs.

These "two lands" were so distinct that the Egyptians themselves gave them two separate names. The valley of Upper Egypt was called *ta-shema,* which means "the Land of the Shema-Reed." *Ta-mehu,* "the Land of the Papyrus-Plant," was the name for the delta of Lower Egypt. How and why these two cultures merged is still not completely known, but researchers do know enough to create a good picture of what predynastic life in each area might have been like.

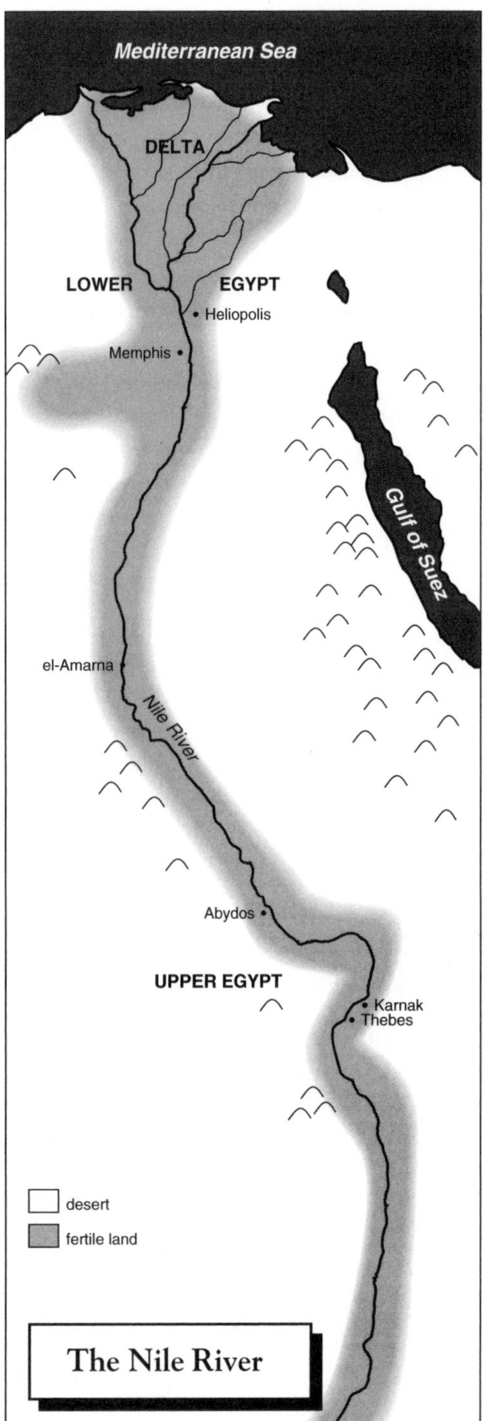

The Nile River

The Badarians

About 4000 B.C. a group of people called the Badarians, who lived near what is today an area called El Badâri, thrived in Upper Egypt. It is unclear where the Badarians came from or whether they simply evolved from an earlier culture. But they were, in many ways, a distinct precursor to the later unified Egyptian civilization. Hoffman points out that "our overall impression of the Badarian culture . . . is one of a developing farming and herding society . . . which foreshadows in technology, economy, and custom later Predynastic cultures and early pharaonic civilizations."[5]

The Badarians were farmers who cultivated the rich land along the Nile River. They lived in permanent villages and relied on farming and domesticated animals for survival. Little is known about the kinds of houses they lived in, but most archaeologists believe they lived in tents made of animal skins. They also wore animal skins instead of cloth, suggesting that they might have migrated to Egypt from a cooler climate. Furthermore, the remains of grains and plants in their villages, along with the remains of animal bones, show that the Badarians ate quite well.

The Badarians were unique because their cultural objects demonstrate a huge leap in two areas: technology and religion. They created amazing pottery that shows a remarkable level of technological skill. The pottery that existed before the Badarians was thick and crude. Badarian pottery, on the other hand, was hard and thin, suggesting that they had a greater skill and understanding of making and firing pottery. Their artistic tastes were also more highly evolved, for they decorated their pottery with colors and polished the pots to a fine shine.

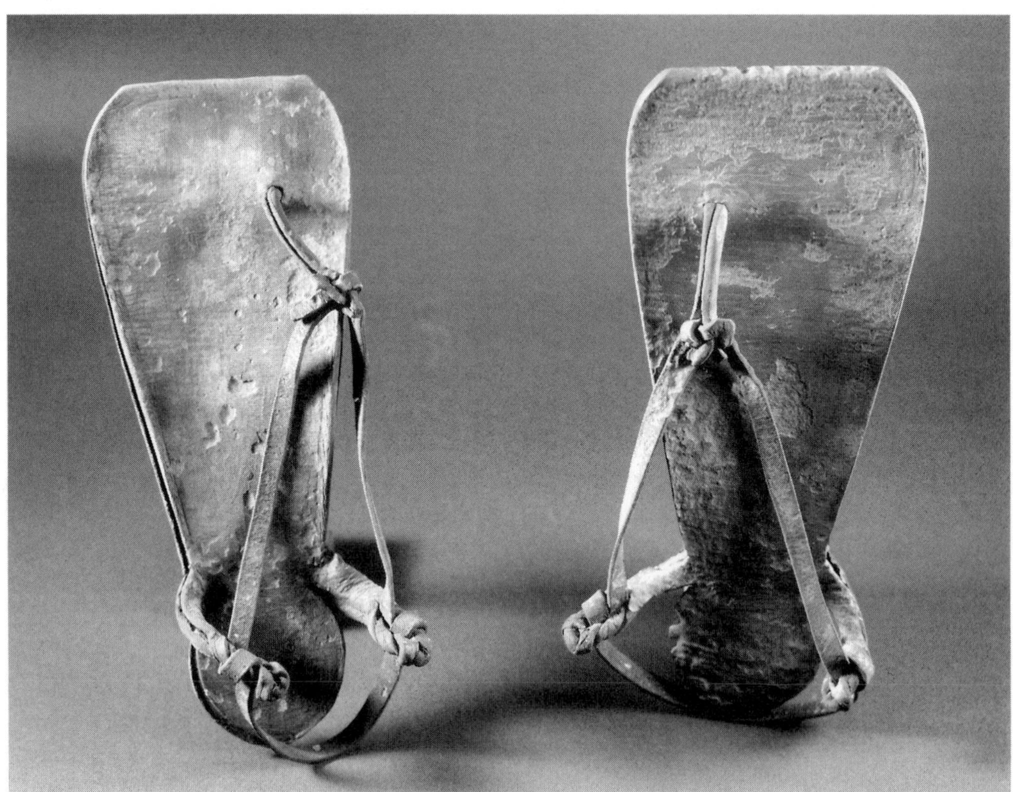

These Egyptian leather sandals date back to the Predynastic era. Their quality of workmanship suggests a developed culture.

Although nothing is known of specific Badarian religious practices, their graves are clues to the role that spiritual beliefs might have played in their lives. Badarian graves were carefully dug oval pits that contained precious objects such as beautiful jewelry and household items. The dead were also buried with baked clay human and animal figures, suggesting some kind of religious worship. These objects show that the Badarians believed in some sort of afterlife. The practice of burying objects with the dead, although still in its earliest stages, evolved to become part of the religious belief system that would fill the great Egyptian kings' tombs with vast treasures in later centuries.

The Amratians

The Badarians flourished in Upper Egypt for about a thousand years. Gradually, however, their culture gave way to another, even richer predynastic civilization, called the Amratians, who lived near the modern site of El-Amra. This culture, also known as Naqada I, was a farming culture, too, but the Amratians were vastly different from the Badarians who came before them.

Amratian village sites reveal that these people lived in circular beehive-shaped houses made of a mixture of mud, limestone chips, and limestone blocks with roofs of straw and reeds. They built outbuildings to store grain and house their farm animals. Some houses in the villages were larger than others, suggesting that someone of greater importance (a chief or a holy man, perhaps) lived there. This in turn points to a society in which there was some form of organized leadership and reverence for those leaders.

Many Amratians lived in a flourishing settlement known as Nubet, which means "the Town of Gold." Little is known about the religious beliefs of the Amratians, but they probably had a complex religious system that may have included a number of gods. Archaeologists have found shrines that the Amratians may have used to worship their gods. These shrines, small and crude as they are, appear to be precursors to the later grand Egyptian temples.

The Amratians, like the Badarians, produced exquisite pottery, revealing an even more complex technological skill. The Amratians took a great deal of joy in decorating their pottery, for much of it is covered with painted scenes from everyday life. These images, like the pots themselves, reveal a great deal about predynastic culture. The paintings show hunters and their weapons, fishermen plying the Nile in their reed boats, and dancers. These decorations convey powerful images of predynastic life and show that these people were part of a vibrant society.

Naqada II

The Amratians gave way to an even more developed predynastic culture known as Naqada II. The Naqada II culture rose about 3800 B.C., and all of the evidence suggests that it was a time of great advancement and excitement in the world. Historian Michael Rice is almost gleeful when he reports that "the Naqada II phase of Egyptian later prehistory is one which was crucial for the formation of the Pharaonic or dynastic state. . . . The essential, peculiarly Egyptian character of the society was emerging very powerfully."[6]

During Naqada II, culture exploded in every imaginable area. The small settlements founded in Amratian times grew, and some became full-fledged cities. Artisans and craftspeople produced increasingly complex and beautiful

This Naqada vase dating back to 4000–3100 B.C. is representative of the complex and beautiful objects created by early Egyptian artisans and craftspeople.

objects, and pottery drawings show a myriad of colorful and detailed designs.

Towns that thrived during this time had cemeteries with lavish burials. The people of Naqada II also believed in stocking graves with grave goods. Many of the burial traditions of the dynastic Egyptians evolved directly from the practices of the Naqada II. Rice describes their tombs as minihomes filled with everything that the dead could ever need—a custom that later became synonymous with the Egyptians. He says,

> The deceased were laid on reed mats and invariably accompanied by grave offerings that reflected their relative wealth and aspects of their daily life: tools such as flint knives, scrapers, and arrowheads; green slate grinding palettes with accompanying malachite or hematite pigment stones; copper punches, awls, and adzes; [imported] ornaments like shell and stone beads; containers fashioned from stones . . . ; and a bewildering variety of fine, handmade polished red ware and black-topped red ware jars as well as more enigmatic artifacts that throw light on individual differences and personal preferences, like baked clay figurines, amulets, and carved ivory plaques.[7]

The People of Lower Egypt

Although a great deal of archaeological evidence has been uncovered in Upper Egypt, little is known about the people who lived in predynastic Lower Egypt. For decades, the Nile delta region has been an inhospitable place to conduct any archaeological work because of the terrain. Lower Egyptian sites are usually situated near the riverbank, and a great deal of archaeological evidence has been washed away by flooding.

Archaeologists are also hindered because predynastic people built their small farming villages on rises near the river, surrounded by miles of empty land for farming. As the years passed, the villages grew by building on top of their own debris. This building tradition creates tremendous problems in finding evidence of the earliest cultures, Rice says, because "in Lower Egypt, not only are many ancient cities buried beneath modern successors, but they have often been robbed for building materials, or pushed farther down into marshy subsoil by the overburden and the alluvial deposit of millennia."[8]

Although there is little evidence, archaeologists have found the remains of cultures that thrived in Lower Egypt, and they were most likely just as strong as those in the south. One of them, Merimde beni Salame, has been a treasure house of information about predynastic life in Lower Egypt.

The Merimdens

One of the largest Lower Egyptian predynastic settlements lies about thirty-seven miles (sixty kilometers) north of modern-day Cairo. Scholars believe that people settled in the modern-day area, now called Merimde beni Salame, in about 4800 B.C. and lived there for more than six hundred years.

The people of Merimde built their town on a rise near the Nile, to protect them from the river's yearly life-giving floods. Merimde was a large settlement, crowding as many as five thousand people into a compact town. The townspeople lived in oval-shaped houses clustered together randomly. They ground grains to make breads and other foods, and they made baskets to store their foodstuffs. Like the homes of the people of Upper Egypt, the ruins of permanent houses imply that the Merimdens were a farming community and relied more on growing crops than traveling to hunt and gather their food.

However, the greatest clues to the Merimdens' culture lie in their burials. Although their burial customs were similar to those of the people in Upper Egypt, almost none of the Merimdens' graves contained grave goods.

COMMON TRAITS OF PREDYNASTIC EGYPTIANS

Although two separate cultures grew and thrived in the predynastic era of Egyptian history, there is much about the two groups that is alike. It is believed that predynastic peoples shared a language, for there is evidence that they traded goods back and forth. Pottery fragments from the north appear in villages far to the south, and similar imported goods from far outside Egyptian borders are found in many predynastic villages of both Upper and Lower Egypt.

It is also possible that these cultures influenced one another's religious beliefs. Although Lower Egyptian graves are empty of goods, the bodies are usually turned toward the south, with their faces turned westward. Upper Egyptian burials also show this position. West became the direction of the dead in dynastic times, and all Egyptians were buried in this fashion. No one knows when or where the tradition began, but its use throughout predynastic Egypt hints that it developed in one area and was adopted by another. The people of both areas also wrapped and buried their dead, suggesting that some of their spiritual beliefs might have been similar.

This is a striking departure from the rest of Egyptian culture. The Merimdens also did not have an organized cemetery. Rather, they buried their dead within the town. Archaeologists cannot explain these differences. Little else is known about the Merimdens.

Hierakonpolis, the First City

For more than one thousand years—from about 4000 to 3000 B.C.—the people of Upper and Lower Egypt lived separately. The Merimdens grew their crops and watched the yearly rise and fall of the Nile. To the south, the people of Naqada II painted their pottery and held elaborate burials for their dead. As time went on, however, changes began. Small villages became large towns. Although researchers are unsure how it happened, they think that a combination of good leadership, successful crops, and a healthy economy helped some towns rise to power. By about the year 3200 B.C. one Egyptian town had become a full-fledged city. The ancient Egyptians called it Nekhen. Today it is known by the name the Greeks gave it, Hierakonpolis, or "City of the Falcon," for the hawk god, Horus, whom the residents worshiped.

Most archaeologists consider Hierakonpolis to be the first capital of Egypt. They base that idea on a number of things, the most important of which is the city's age. Since it dates from about 3100, the time that Egypt was unified, it is reasonable to assume that it was one of the first. At about this time, for some unknown reason, the population of Hierakonpolis rose sharply, creating a burst of growth that likely enabled it to become an urban center. It was probably militarily important, for the city is enclosed by a mighty stone wall and includes a massive gateway that was built both as a fortification and as a grand city beautification project. Inside the wall was a grand temple, one of the oldest ever discovered in Egypt. No other city in Egypt of its time could compare to it.

Researchers do not know what life was like in this town. No records or stories have survived to reveal who the people of Hierakonpolis were or how they went about their daily lives. However, the city thrived for centuries as the center of society and probably as the center for Horus worship. It was revered by later pharaohs as the symbolic home of the god Horus.

Despite its importance, the city did not survive the ages, although historians are not sure why Hierakonpolis declined. One widely held belief is that the city's importance as an urban center faded and that the population gradually moved to other, more exciting towns. What is certain is that when the Egyptian civilization fell, rulers focused their attention on other places, leaving Hierakonpolis to be buried beneath new construction.

Rediscovering Hierakonpolis

For centuries, Hierakonpolis lay hidden and undisturbed. Then, in 1897, amidst the frenzy of the new science of Egyptology, two English archaeologists named James Quibell and Frederick Green arrived in Egypt. Quibell, a recent college graduate, wanted to make a name for himself, and he decided he would do it by searching for Hierakonpolis.

The city would not be hard to find. Historian Hoffman explains that, "despite the fact that the town had lain almost completely deserted for over 4,000 years, pharaohs down through the ages had continued to heap gifts

DIGGING AT HIERAKONPOLIS

James Quibell conducted two archaeological digs at the ancient city of Hierakonpolis in 1897–1898 and 1898–1899. His accounts of the finds at the dig illustrate the excitement—and the backbreaking labor—that went into archaeological work. In this quote, from Dennis Forbes's article entitled "Quibell at Hierakonpolis," he describes finding a cache of objects.

"[They were] apparently of the earliest historical period. They lay at a low level, below all the existing walls of the temple. . . . Here there was a small rise of about 2 meters [about 7 feet] in the ground. . . . When this mound was cleared a group of chambers was disclosed, the contents of which were not important; but as the walls did not rest on undisturbed sand we went down deeper, and just below the level of the walls began to come upon scattered objects of the archaic period.

There were two sharp-edged stone maces, a flint knife, and a vase with a large conical seal of yellow clay. . . . More than twenty objects, all of archaic types, were found lying together: a green glaze monkey, a large quartz mace, and some pieces of inscribed ivory. . . . There was also a great heap made up entirely of objects in ivory, chiefly statuettes. . . .

Day after day we sat in this hole, scraping away the earth, and trying to disentangle the objects from one another; for they lay in every possible position, each piece being in contact with five or six others, interlocking as a handful of matches will, when shaken together and thrown down upon the table."

and honors upon the home of the legendary founder of their line and his patron god, Horus of Nekhen."[9]

Quibell and Green focused their attention on the city's temple, which was one of the earliest temples dedicated to an Egyptian god. Almost immediately they discovered object after ancient object in the ruins, and they soon realized the magnitude of their find. As Quibell later said, "[The find] . . . contained a great number of objects, apparently from the earliest historical period. . . . There were two sharp-edged stone maces, a flint knife, and a vase with a large conical seal of yellow clay. . . . More than twenty objects, all of archaic types, were found together."[10]

Quibell and Green's most significant find was a simple piece of slate, carved on both sides with pictures. Called the Narmer palette, it was one of the most important Egyptian finds ever to surface because it depicted the unification of Upper and Lower Egypt under one ruler.

An important archaeological discovery, the Narmer palette depicts, and perhaps confirms, the unification of Upper and Lower Egypt.

On one side of the palette was an image of a man wearing the red crown of Lower Egypt. He gazes at a row of dead bodies on a battlefield as a scribe and a row of flag bearers walk before him. A set of hieroglyphs give the king's name: Narmer. On the other side of the palette, the same figure wears the white crown of Upper Egypt. He is grasping an enemy by the hair with one hand and holds a clublike weapon with the other, raised to deliver a killing blow.

Since the earliest days of Egyptian civilization, the people believed that Upper and Lower Egypt had been unified by one king. Until Quibell and Green, however, no one had any proof. To many archaeologists, the Narmer palette confirmed that there had indeed been an Egyptian king who united the two lands into one kingdom.

With this unification there was no longer an Upper and Lower Egypt, each with its own separate culture, burial practices, and lifestyles. The great Egyptian civilization had begun.

Chapter Two

The King and His People

To the Egyptians, the land was everything. Their lives depended solely on the life-giving Nile and the black soil that nursed their crops. The various predynastic cultures rose as they tamed the land by farming and by raising animals. They also began praying to gods and goddesses whom they believed controlled their world by controlling the land and everything on it. This control was vital, because they believed that any disruption in the normal workings of nature could create chaos, starvation, and death.

By the time of the first kings, the concepts of land, gods, and life were interchangeable. In the first centuries of dynastic Egypt, these three powerful concepts coalesced, or came together, in one person: the king. The king controlled everything in Egypt, and he became first a symbolic, and then an actual, god. As one historian explains,

> The role of the king is central to Egyptian belief in order and remains, until the arrival of Christianity, one of the four inseparable core strands of Pharaonic civilization, together with art, writing, and religion. From the earliest written sources the king stands at the center of his country as a divine force, identified in his first name and title as a manifestation of the god of power.[11]

However, the king was only one person, and the country was far too vast for him to

Ancient Egyptian artwork emphasizes the society's dependence on farming and the Nile River to provide sustenance and life.

oversee personally. As a result, he had to delegate his authority to others. Slowly, a government structure called a bureaucracy formed to handle the maintenance of the land. This eventually evolved into the complex, controlled web of Egyptian society that became the base of the culture's foundation.

The King Is Considered to Be God

During most of the time of the Egyptian civilization, the king was indelibly linked with the powerful gods in whom the Egyptians believed. No one knows for sure how or when this correlation began. Some scholars believe it was rooted in the ancient belief that gods and spirits once created and ruled Egypt before mankind. Others suggest that the warrior king who finally unified Upper and Lower Egypt was seen as a god by the people. Still others contend that the first kings linked themselves with the local gods of more powerful villages, creating an association with a popular god to bring more power and respect to themselves. Regardless of how the beliefs began, however, even the earliest written sources depict the king as a god.

An Egyptian text describes the king, and its eloquent words and reverent tone reveal some of the feelings that Egyptians had for their ruler:

> His eyes probe every being. . . . He illuminates the Two Lands (Upper and Lower Egypt) more than the sun disk. . . . He makes (things) green more than a great inundation. He fills the Two Lands with strength and life. Noses grow cold when he falls into a rage; when he is calmed, one breathes the air. He ensures the sustenance of those who follow him. . . . His enemy will be impoverished.[12]

To the Egyptians, the king was the earthly incarnation of the hawk god, Horus. As historians Douglas Brewer and Emily Teeter write, "Mythologically, all kings were considered to be descendants of the early gods. Each king was the incarnation of the god Horus. . . . Even kings who were acknowledged to be of non-royal blood assumed the mythical mantle of Horus."[13]

Horus was one of the most powerful Egyptian gods, and one of the most common Horus myths describes how Horus and another god, Seth, battled for power over Egypt. One version of the myth is included in a document called the "Memphite Theology," and it explains that it was Horus who united the two lands of Egypt:

> [Geb, lord of the gods] judged between Horus and Seth; he ended their quarrel. He made Seth king of Upper Egypt . . . and he made Horus king of Lower Egypt. . . . Thus Horus stood over one region and Seth stood over one region. They made peace over the Two Lands at Ayan. That was the division of the Two Lands. . . . Then it seemed wrong to Geb that the portion of Horus was like the portion of Seth. So . . . Geb said, "I have appointed Horus, the firstborn." . . . He is Horus who arose as King of Upper and Lower Egypt, who united the Two Lands in the Nome of the Wall (Memphis), the place in which the Two Lands were united.[14]

Although the king's link with Horus is undisputed at the beginning of the dynastic era, it

KING LISTS

The Egyptians did not leave any comprehensive histories of their civilization. What they did create, however, were what are now known as king lists, which chronicled each king and queen and his or her reign throughout history. These lists show the rise and fall of certain rulers, but they also reveal the reverence and awe that the Egyptians had for those who sat on the throne of Egypt.

One of the most famous temple king lists in existence today is inscribed in the Gallery of the Lists in the temple of King Seti I. This impressive list covers an entire wall of the temple and shows images of King Seti I and his son Ramses II, making an offering to seventy-six royal ancestors.

Although archaeologists today use king lists to study Egyptian history, the Egyptians themselves used the lists for a very different purpose. The priests used the king lists in rituals that honored the king in whose temple the list was inscribed. Each day, a ritual called the Ritual of the Royal Ancestors was performed in these temples. First, the priests retrieved the food and other offerings that had been placed at the statue of the god of the temple. These offerings were brought to the room where the king list was located and offered to the kings on the list; the Egyptians believed that such an offering would ensure that the dead kings would bestow blessings on the owner of the temple.

Today, archaeologists compare the names on the king lists with artifacts they find in order to determine who lived when and to identify objects associated with specific rulers. Because of these king lists, archaeologists have a very good idea about who ruled Egypt and the importance of the king in the fabric of society.

Archaeologists rely on king lists to document ancient Egyptian rulers. A famous lineage is inscribed in the Gallery of the Lists in the temple of King Seti I (pictured).

is unknown how the ruler became associated with the gods in the earliest days. What is certain, however, is that kings were associated with Horus from the earliest days of Egyptian civilization. According to historian Barry Kemp,

> The name Horus—which means "The One on High"—may have had widespread currency within religious experience throughout Predynastic Egypt. . . . If we turn to archaeology we can find a limited amount of evidence for kingly associations with Horus in the earlier periods. . . . Horus is one deity whose figure appears unambiguously [absolutely] in association with Early Dynastic kings.[15]

Society and the King

In theory, the king was responsible for all activities in Egypt. He was the only landholder, the only priest, the only warrior, and the only judge. Because he was considered to be a god, Egyptians believed that he had the power to control every aspect of life. Furthermore, the king was set apart from the rest of society, and his life of splendor must have seemed godlike to the common people.

Thirteenth-century B.C. *Egyptian pharaoh Ramses II receives imperial power from the gods Seth (left) and Horus (right).*

Beneath this belief in the all-powerful king was a deeper desire—the need for control and structure in the world. The desire for control began with the land, which the Egyptians believed was owned by the king. The king could relinquish the land to other institutions, such as temples and cities, but it, in theory, remained his property and his responsibility. Private citizens and government organizations such as temples could own property, and even buy and sell it, but it was not legal ownership. This was known as usufruct (the right to enjoy what the land produced).

Those who worked the land did so for the king, and the king received payment in return. This payment was in the form of taxes, and an entire bureaucracy was created to keep track of the land's yield, or production, and to collect the taxes. This land-based bureaucracy became the basis of the entire Egyptian society. The complex and far-reaching government that grew powerful during the rise of Egyptian civilization did so as a result of this quest to control the natural world.

The basis of government organization in Egypt was the nome. Egypt was divided into forty-two districts, called nomes. The earliest record of the existence of nomes dates to the Old Kingdom era (2686–2181 B.C.), but some historians believe that Egypt was divided into nomelike districts even in its earliest days. Nomes were very similar to a state in the United States, and each nome had its own treasury, courts of law, maintenance offices, scribes, and military.

Nomes were governed by a local official called a *nomarche*. This official, similar to a modern governor, had a staff that ran the day-to-day business of the nome. *Nomarches* were members of the ruling class, and they lived aristocratic lives. The importance of the *nomarches* is clear, for many of them were given titles and allowed to build their own tombs alongside the royal tombs. This high honor was reserved for the most important members of society, and the mere existence of such tombs points to the fact that *nomarches* were highly respected and admired. But the *nomarches* were not rulers, they were officials with close ties to the central government. Representatives of the king regularly visited the nomes and assessed the land for taxes. In this way, the king maintained control over the land.

Early in Egyptian civilization the position of *nomarche* became hereditary, which means that the office was passed down from father to son in a family. This practice enabled the *nomarches* to hold great power over their nomes. In later times the *nomarches* grew stronger, and some even competed with the king for power. As a result, during the Middle Kingdom era (2040–1782 B.C.) the position of *nomarche* was abolished due to the fact that *nomarches* became a threat to the security of the kingship.

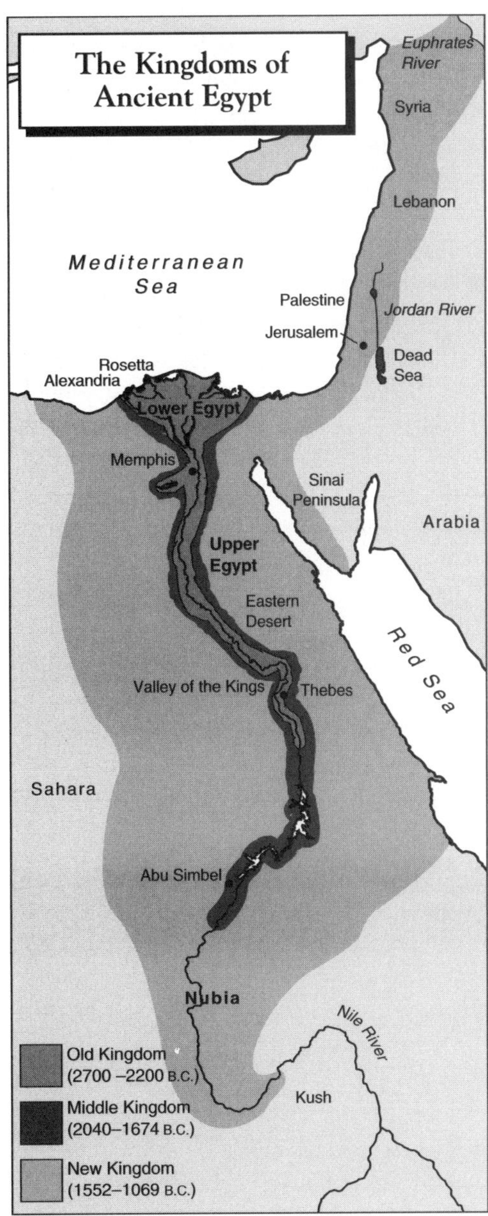

The Vizier: Eyes and Ears of the King

The second in command of Egyptian society was a high government official called the vizier. This title is comparable to the office of vice president or prime minister, and the vizier was second only to the king in prestige and power.

Of all the responsibilities of the vizier, the most important was controlling the people who made the government work. The vizier, sometimes referred to as "the ears and eyes of the king," had a great many duties. Chief among those was to maintain civil order, assess and collect taxes, maintain public records, mobilize troops if needed, appoint lower government officials, and review laws and legal claims. Sometimes the vizier also served as mayor of a city in addition to his other jobs.

The king chose his vizier, and the two men were usually friends who shared a close relationship. Many of them wrote to one another, sending orders and responses back and forth. One letter, sent from King Djedkare-Izezi to a vizier by the name of Senedjemib, reveals the close relationship that a vizier might have with his king. The letter reads,

> My Majesty [the King] knows that you are more skillful than any overseer of works who has ever been in the entire land. . . .You have indeed achieved distinction innumerable times, so you shall serve as overseer of all works of the king. O Senedjemib Senior, it is with me that I want you to be, for you know full well that I love you.[16]

The job of vizier was a difficult, all-consuming one. It sometimes became so overwhelming that two or three viziers had to be appointed to oversee different lands or specific aspects of government. When this happened, the viziers might live in different Egyptian cities and divide the duties of the office among them. For example, there were two viziers during the New Kingdom (1570–1069 B.C). One oversaw all of Lower Egypt and lived in the city of Memphis. The vizier of Upper Egypt resided in Thebes and also traveled throughout the area.

As the civilization progressed, the tasks of the vizier changed, but he remained one of the most important people in Egyptian society. Far from being a glorious position, however, the job of vizier was one of the most demanding roles in government. It was not an exaggeration when one Egyptian text described the vizier's role by saying, "Assume the office of vizier, attend to everything that is done in its name; for it is the support of the whole land. Indeed, the vizierate is not sweet; it is bitter as bile."[17]

Other Government Officials

Below the vizier were a dizzying number of individual government departments and offices, each charged with its own task within the society. Little is known about the different kinds of offices that ran Egypt or what their specific purposes were. Many are known today only by the titles of the department heads, such as overseer of the treasury, overseer of all of the the king's works, overseer of the king's documents, overseer of the granaries, and overseer of the army. These titles suggest a huge, well-run bureaucracy that was carefully controlled and organized.

Although there is little information about the specific departments of Egyptian government, its sheer size indicates that it was one of the most important aspects of the Egyptian civilization. Each department in the government employed many people who historians believe had specific duties. However, it is unclear what these duties were since many of the titles eventually became honorary titles in later times.

The magnitude of the Egyptian bureaucracy affected all parts of Egyptian civilization, for it existed as a vehicle for the king to keep track of his lands. As historians Brewer and Teeter illustrate, "The bureaucracy touched all aspects of Egyptian life in its quest to assess taxes, collect the prescribed amount of grain, store it, and distribute it to finance the works of state and temple."[18]

Priests, Temples, and Scribes

The king, in theory, was the head of all temples. He was the direct liaison with the gods, and it was his responsibility to give offerings to each god every day. As a god himself, the king was the only person in Egyptian society who conversed with the gods directly and intervened on behalf of the people. In practice, however, the king could not personally give offerings in each temple, to each god, at all times of the day. Priests became the king's representatives to the gods. As the Egyptian civilization grew and flourished, priests and the gods they worshiped became entwined in the daily structure of Egyptian society.

TITLES OF THE KING

To the Egyptians, the king was at the core of their culture and their religious beliefs. He was the embodiment of all of the power and control they craved. As the kingship grew in importance, its association with gods became stronger. By the Fifth Dynasty, the king had five royal titles, and they show how closely the king was linked with the Egyptian gods.

The king's first title was written inside a panel that represented the palace, which showed the king and Horus alive in the palace walls. The word for palace was *per-aa*, from which the biblical word *pharaoh* is derived. The second title was *nebty*, which means "He of the Two Ladies." This title referred to the fact that the king was protected by two powerful goddesses, the cobra-goddess Wadjyt of Lower Egypt and the vulture-goddess Nekhbet of Upper Egypt. The third title translated into "Horus of Gold." The fourth title, *nesut bity*, translated into "the Ruler of the Upper and Lower Regions."

Gradually, kings became closely associated with more powerful deities. The belief that the king was the son of the great sun god Ra emerged during the Old Kingdom. It was at this time that the fifth title, "the Son of Ra," (or Re) began to appear with a king's name.

Throughout the remainder of Egyptian history, the king carried these titles. But more importantly, the people deeply believed that the king was a god, so these titles were more than mere names. They were the proof that their king was all-powerful, and that he controlled every aspect of the Egyptian world.

This mural painting on an Egyptian tomb portrays the important religious ceremony of pouring sacred water and carrying incense to appease the gods.

The temples of Egypt were more than places of worship. They were part of the vast, controlled organization of religion. In the early centuries, temples were literally the houses of gods. Priests cared for each god's house and made offerings to the deity who lived there. The offerings came from the land owned by the temple, and this encouraged priests to acquire more land and resources for the gods. As a result, temples eventually controlled thousands of acres, oversaw the cultivation of crops, and were taxed just as other groups were. A large portion of Egypt's economy relied on the temples and the lands they worked in the name of the king and the gods. Historian Barry Kemp describes the system, revealing that

> temple land [was] subdivided into an elaborate tapestry of holdings, some cultivated by temple agents, and others by people who cover almost the entire spectrum of Egyptian society, from small farmers cultivating on their own behalf through priests and soldiers, to the vizier himself, these latter groups being clearly landlords employing laborers. . . . Other forms of agricultural holding donated to temples included animal herds, fish-

> ing and fowling rights, flax fields to provide the raw material from which linen garments were manufactured in temple workshops, vegetable beds, vineyards, and beehives.[19]

Temples with large landholdings were valuable to the government, and the priests who ran them had a great deal of influence. Sometimes the temple priest would be one of the most powerful people in an Egyptian town.

Some of the economically stronger temples served as a kind of government department rather than a religious organization, especially if the god whom the temple worshiped happened to be a popular or powerful one. The priests of a god who was widely worshiped, for example, might be able to sway public opinion for or against a political issue. The king who gave his favor to a certain temple could rely on that temple's resources and taxes as a source of income as well.

The Temple Staff

Temples were tightly controlled, just like the rest of Egyptian society. A temple's staff was organized into an administration as structured and as complex as the government's. The highest priestly position in the temple was that of a prophet. Prophets were ranked in numerical order, with the first prophet being the most important. The position of first prophet was one of great responsibility, and this person controlled a vast network of employees. For example, the first prophet of the temple of Amun, during the time of King Ramses II (1304–1237 B.C.), oversaw eighty-one thousand people in the service of that god, a figure that also included those who worked on the vast tracts of land that the temple owned.

Below the prophets were other ranks of priests. The *khery-hebet,* or lector priests, read religious texts. The *sem* priests cared for goods such as fabric, perfume, and other items that were used in offerings. *Iwenmutef* priests officiated at funerals. Priests with titles such as overseer of the prophets, inspector of the prophets, or fathers of the god took care of the managerial details of temple life. There was also a large population of priests called *wab,* or all purpose priests.

As the elaborate architecture of this pylon indicates, Egyptian temples were considered not just places of worship, but actual homes for the gods.

The foundation of this rigid hierarchy was the underlying belief that everything in the gods' world was systematic, predictable, and comforting. The lives of the priests who tended to the gods' needs reflected this belief in the smallest details, including personal hygiene and clothing. Priests were meticulous about the way they lived, reflecting the attitude of structure that pervaded society as well as the idea that the servants of the gods had to maintain a certain level of reverence to their deities. The Greek historian Herodotus described the Egyptian priesthood and the priests that he met during his travels in the fifth-century B.C., writing that

> priests shave every part of their bodies every other day, to stop themselves [from] getting lice or in general being at all unclean as they minister to the gods. The priests wear only one garment made out of linen, while their shoes are papyrus; they are not allowed to wear any other kind of clothing or footwear, and they wash with cold water twice every day and twice at night too. It is hardly an exaggeration to say that the priests practice thousands upon thousands of other religious observances. However, they gain plenty of benefits as well; they do not have anything of their own to wear out or to consume, but even their food, which is sacred, is cooked for them; each of them is also provided with a generous daily allowance of beef and goose-meat, and their wine is donated as well. . . . Each deity has a number of priests, not just one, though there is a single high priest in each case; when a priest dies, his son is appointed in his place.[20]

Scribes

Temples could not give offerings to the gods if they did not know what kinds of offerings they had. Likewise, the king could not collect taxes without records. The role of recorder and information specialist fell to the scribes. Scribes recorded every aspect of Egyptian life and were the mortar that held the bricks of Egyptian society together. They were some of the few literate members of Egyptian civilization, and the ability to read and write was one of the most respected goals a person could achieve. As historians Douglas Brewer and Emily Teeter explain,

> Literacy was highly prized in ancient Egypt because it was the means of advancement between social classes and within the government bureaucracy. Yet in spite of the emphasis placed upon writing and literacy, during most of Egyptian history probably no more than 1 percent of the population was literate. . . . Thus, the scribal class was highly esteemed.[21]

Although few became well known or famous, scribes were one of the most vital components of Egyptian society. They helped maintain the strict control and flow of everyday life by providing the basic information—inventories—that kept the rest of Egyptian society running smoothly. Brewer and Teeter further illustrate this point:

> Numerous texts and tomb scenes demonstrate how the managerial and auditing function of the scribes entered into the people's daily life. Everything was noted: size of herds, amount of grain harvested, amounts

of seed-grain and materials issued from store, types and quantities of objects manufactured, building supplies, and tools and artisan supplies requested. . . . Although listing all that was produced, crafted, and captured throughout Egypt seems pedantic [scholarly], scribal records provided an account of Egyptian stocks and reserves and made taxation and eventual redistribution of goods possible.[22]

The Scribe's Job

In the earliest days of the Egyptian civilization, scribes were little more than government workers, tracking and recording the yearly crops and animal herds for the king. Gradually, however, as the bureaucracy grew and expanded, it was vital that the king have complete, accurate records of all of the items that the land produced. The king also needed to know how many people were in Egypt, their professions, and many other particulars of his

The government's representatives to the common people, scribes (represented in this carving) recorded the details of Egyptian life and gave order to it.

The hieroglyphs were the Egyptians' form of writing and have become the tools that archaeologists rely on today to study the ancient society.

subjects' lives. The scribes who recorded these details of Egyptian life became an integral part of Egyptian society.

Everything, including wills, deeds, population lists, lists of military personnel, orders, tax lists, letters, journals, inventories, purchase orders, royal requests, temple records, and trial transcripts were recorded. Thousands of scribes spent their entire lives in the service of the government, yet a scribe was more than a mere record keeper. The position demanded people who were intelligent, independent, and good managers. They gave orders, took meticulous records, and handled most aspects of the business world. The scribes were a vital part of the Egyptian civilization. They gave order to the natural chaos of daily life. Furthermore, their jobs, and the lives of many ordinary people, depended on them.

The scribe was also the one government worker with whom most ordinary Egyptians came in contact on a daily basis. As such, scribes were the government's official representatives to the common people. They made wills, recorded marriage contracts, and drew up contracts and other financial arrangements. They also made lists of animal herds, harvested grain, building materials, and even work attendance records and wages paid to workers.

Additionally, scribes were the only members of Egyptian society who were fluent in the use of hieroglyphs, but not all scribes learned to read and write them. As historian Christine Hobson relates,

> Learning to write hieroglyphs, rather than hieratic [a less complex form of writing], was the province of the selected few. Those scribes who were finally apprenticed to stonemasons, carpenters, and painters, would have to learn exactly how to draw hieroglyphs within a marked grid so that painters could transfer them onto walls.[23]

Hieroglyphs were used on monuments, temples, government documents, and religious papyri as the formal language of the society. The earliest hieroglyphs were created in the first years of the archaic period (3150–2686 B.C.), when scribes used a combination of pictures and numbers to record the possessions of the king. Soon there was a need for a more complex form of writing, and more pictures were added. For personal documents such as contracts, wills, and other documents, scribes developed a form of writing called hieratic, which was less complex and could be written faster than hieroglyphs.

The Effects of Control on Society

The Egyptians' craving for order and control might seem constricting at first glance. The vast network of government officials, priests, and scribes was, in fact, an intricately developed system that allowed for very little (if any) change. However, for centuries the Egyptian civilization thrived and grew to unimaginable power because of the people's belief in an ordered, structured world. The Egyptian people had found a system that worked, and each person understood his or her place in it. Because everyone believed that order was vital for life, they strove to achieve it in everything they did. For many years, they succeeded.

Chapter Three

The Glory of Egypt: The Old Kingdom

When most people think of ancient Egypt, they think of the majestic pyramids that have stood against the backdrop of desert and shimmering heat for centuries. These structures symbolize the glory that was the Egyptian civilization, and they were as marvelous and impressive when they were first built as they are today.

The pyramids were constructed during the Old Kingdom, which lasted from 2686 to 2181 B.C. This is the period of Egyptian history that is commonly referred to as its golden age, and during that time, the recently unified country created structures of such splendor and majesty that they have never been equaled.

For historians, the Old Kingdom represents the greatness of ancient Egypt. According to historian Michael Rice, "The high point of the ancient Egyptian contribution to the civilization of the world and one of the highest points of human experience thus far achieved by our peculiar species, is to be found in the period known as 'the Old Kingdom.'"[24]

It was a time of almost unparalleled achievement in religion, art, culture, and architecture. Religious rituals were established and became the standard for everything that came afterward. Funerary practices, including the making of mummies, flourished during this time. The economy grew strong, and it was a time of peace and prosperity for the Egyptian people.

In the center of it all was the king, who ruled not only the Egyptian society but controlled the entire universe. He was surrounded by an ever-expanding governmental system that maintained the order of the land. Together they created some of the most spectacular things that the Egyptian civilization ever achieved. The most significant, and the objects that best symbolize their lost culture, are the great pyramids.

Tombs of the Kings

The Old Kingdom is known as the golden age of the pyramids because this era saw the construction of the first pyramids ever built. Dozens of pyramids are known today, although many of them are little more than piles of rubble. A few, however, such as the famous pyramids of Giza, still stand as majestic reminders of this time in Egyptian history. All of the pyramids were built as burial places of the kings of Egypt, and most of them were constructed between 2700 and 1640 B.C.

The evolution of the pyramids took many centuries. In predynastic times, people were

PYRAMID BUILDING

The question of how the great pyramids were constructed has been a topic of debate for decades. Greek historian Herodotus was one of the first to describe the construction of a pyramid in his book *The Histories*.

"[Workers] worked in gangs of 100,000 men for three months at a time. They said that it took ten years of hard labor for the people to construct the causeway along which they hauled the blocks of stone, which I would think involved not much less work than building the pyramid, since the road is five stades long, ten fathoms wide, and eight fathoms high at its highest point. The actual pyramid took twenty years to build. . . . The pyramid was built up like a flight of stairs (others use the image of staggered battlements or altar steps). When that first stage of the construction process was over, they used appliances made out of short pieces of wood to lift the remaining blocks of stone up the sides. First they would raise a block of stone from the ground on to the first tier, and when the stone had been raised up to that point, it was put on to a different device which was positioned on the first level, and from there it was hauled up to the second level on another device. . . . They finished off the topmost parts of the pyramid first, then the ones just under it, and ended with the ground levels and the lowest ones."

Scholars believe that about twenty thousand workers participated in the construction of the Egyptian pyramids.

Modern scholars doubt that it took one hundred thousand workers to build the pyramids. They suspect that the number was closer to about twenty thousand. These building sites were full of activity throughout the year, and workers served in rotations. They lived in a workers' village complete with houses, bakeries, breweries, and other necessary businesses of everyday life.

buried in oval pits in the sand along with objects they would need in the afterlife. At the beginning of the dynastic period, about 3100 B.C., it became customary to build a structure over the burial pits of kings and nobility. This structure, which became known as a mastaba, kept the sand from being blown away from the tomb and ensured that the body would be preserved. According to historian Christine Hobson, "The kings of Egypt had been buried in underground chambers at the foot of shafts with the flat, rectangular superstructure of a mastaba tomb over them."[25] The earliest mastabas were only a few square meters, but as religious practices became more evolved, mastabas became more richly decorated.

Imhotep and King Djoser

During the first and second dynasties (a series of kings usually taking the same name) of the Old Kingdom, royalty was still being buried beneath mastabas. Most people expected that King Djoser Netjerykhet, who came to the throne in about 2686 B.C., would be buried the same way. This powerful and charismatic ruler surrounded himself with loyal and intelligent followers, and one of them was his minister and master builder, Imhotep. Imhotep was a brilliant and innovative man whom many historians credit with the idea of the pyramids. Rice explains this, saying, "Imhotep, it is not an exaggeration to suggest, was one of the greatest creative geniuses the human species has yet produced. His achievement dwarfs those of [Athenian sculptor] Praxiteles, Michelangelo, and Leonardo [da Vinci], for what he did no man before him had attempted, nor perhaps even conceived."[26]

When Imhotep began building a royal mastaba for Djoser, his imagination began to shine. Djoser, not surprisingly, wanted his tomb to be magnificent, and Imhotep rose to the challenge. After completing an ornate mastaba, he enlarged it over and over until it became an enormous building with more than ten thousand tons of stone used in its construction.

Then Imhotep got an even grander idea. He enclosed the original mastaba and began to build upward. Slowly, stone by stone, the first pyramid rose toward the heavens. Together, Imhotep and Djoser created what is known as the Step Pyramid, the oldest pyramid in existence today. It was an impressive sight. According to Rice,

> Eventually this first of all pyramids stood 60 meters [197 feet] high [when it was completed]. It contained 850,000 tons of stone excavated for its construction and cut into small blocks; the sheer quantity of stone quarried for the purpose is without precedent. Altogether around one million tons of stone was required for the complex, all, as far as we know, quarried in the king's lifetime. The whole immense structure was cased in fine white limestone; nothing like it had ever before been seen anywhere upon the earth.[27]

The pyramid is called the Step Pyramid because its sides resemble stair steps rather than the smooth sides that are normally associated with pyramids. The Step Pyramid was part of a complex of buildings that, to this day, remains one of the most astounding feats of construction in the world. The outer walls of the complex stretch 1,790 feet (545 meters) north to south and 910 feet (270 meters) east to west. Inside the walls there are huge courtyards, burial chambers, altars, buildings, and statuary devoted to Djoser.

The Pyramids of Giza

The Step Pyramid was only the beginning. The construction of the Step Pyramid began a frenzy of royal pyramid construction that lasted for hundreds of years. For the next few centuries, the kings of Egypt built even grander pyramids for their tombs. The most famous, of course, are the pyramids of Giza.

These three pyramids were built by three kings of the Fourth Dynasty, King Khufu, King Khafre, and King Menkure. The largest, known as the Great Pyramid, was constructed by Khufu. This pyramid, which contains more than 2 million stones of about 2.5 tons each, is the largest stone structure ever built.

One of the most spectacular feats of construction in the world, the Step Pyramid (pictured) was built to honor Djoser.

Outside, the huge blocks of limestone were covered with a smooth limestone casing. This coating can still be seen at the tip of the Great Pyramid. Inside, there were a number of chambers. The lower chamber was cut into the rock of the desert floor. It may have been either the original burial chamber or a decoy chamber to confuse tomb robbers. The central room, or the great gallery, was considered to be the main burial chamber. The gallery has a huge stone roof. Once the king was buried inside the chamber, workers could slide huge stone blocks into place to seal the doorway.

The pyramids at Giza are part of an elaborate tomb complex that is still not completely understood today. No one is sure why Khufu built the Great Pyramid in the way that he did. No records exist of its construction, and the tomb was robbed of its contents almost as soon as the king died. No royal mummy or treasures were ever found there. However, the sheer size of the pyramids and of the temple complex nearby hints at the elaborate religious beliefs that may have been associated with the king and his death.

The Ritual Boat

In the 1950s archaeologists made another stunning find: a disassembled ritual boat buried in the complex at the foot of the pyramids. Historian Hobson says,

> The pit contained . . . 1,224 individual pieces of wood laid carefully in 13 layers, together with ropes for rigging, baskets, and matting. Some parts, such as oars and slender cabin poles, were recognizable, but the majority were not. The overwhelming sense of confusion can be imagined as archaeologists saw for the

The largest of the pyramids, the Great Pyramid remains a mystery to archaeologists; no records exist of its construction.

> first time a huge kit-form boat with no indication of how to put it together.[28]

The significance of the boat is unclear. Some archaeologists maintain that the boat is a symbol of the king's power and point to the Egyptian belief that Re, the sun god, traveled across the sky in his sun boat. Others think that it may have been buried for purely ceremonial reasons, to ferry the dead king's soul to the afterlife.

Religion and Spirituality

Long before kings built massive pyramids, the Egyptians created a complex system of religious beliefs. In fact, one of the highlights of the Old Kingdom was the emergence of the Egyptian religion and its integration into the daily lives of every Egyptian. Although a great many rituals and customs were in place before this time, it was during the Old Kingdom that these disparate beliefs came together into an organized system.

Religion in Egypt mirrored the idea of a complex, unchanging world. If a new god or goddess appeared, or if a new belief or ritual were established, it did not replace an existing deity or belief. Instead, gods and goddesses simply rose and fell in popularity. New beliefs were added to the old beliefs, and nothing was discarded. Myths, stories, and ideas were layered on one another, creating a complex web of religious ideas.

Most of these religious beliefs are closely linked to the natural world. The Egyptians lived by the regular, predictable cycles of the Nile floods and the seasons, and they created deities and beliefs to both explain their world and as an attempt to control it. According to historian A. Rosalie David,

> To the Egyptian mind, there was no change; the universe worked according to a certain pattern governed by principles laid down in primeval times. Egyptians did not question the beliefs which had been handed down to them; they did not desire to change their society. Their main aim throughout their history was to emulate the conditions which they believed had existed at the dawn of creation. . . . It is not surprising that the Egyptians should cling to such beliefs, for their surroundings—the yearly renewal of the seasons which is so apparent in Egypt—must have suggested to them that life was a cyclical process, whose pattern had been established at some far distant date and which would never change.[29]

TAKE TWO MUMMIES AND CALL ME IN THE MORNING

For centuries, mummies were considered to be medicine. Until the nineteenth century, people ate ground-up mummies in the belief that the chemicals used to create them had some mysterious, medicinal power.

Even the word *mummy* has its origins in later times. The Egyptians did not call their wrapped bodies mummies. This term was derived from the Persian-Arabic word *moumiya*, which means "bitumen" or "pitch." Bitumen was a naturally occurring chemical that Arabic physicians believed would cure most ailments. It was used in ancient times the same way as aspirin is used today.

When the first mummies were discovered, they were found to have a hard black coating. Today, we know that this coating was a result of all of the perfumes, unguents, and resins that were used to prepare a body for burial. Then, however, this black coating was misidentified as bitumen. As the natural deposits of this curative chemical were depleted, people turned to Egyptian mummies for the precious substance. From the Middle Ages onward, mummies by the thousands were transported out Egypt, ground up, and used as medicine.

Mummies were still being used as medicine as late as the 1800s. Eventually, however, people discovered that bitumen did not cure sickness, and the market for ground mummy faded away.

Mummies were believed to have medicinal power until the nineteenth century. This mummy of King Ramses II is on display in the Cairo Museum in Egypt.

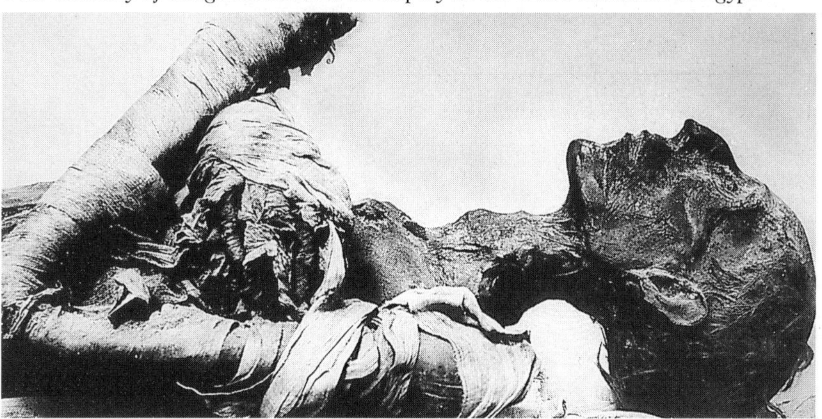

It was not only their belief in a nonchanging world that fueled the Egyptians' religious beliefs. Their connection to nature played an important role as well. As historians Douglas Brewer and Emily Teeter write,

> Most aspects of Egyptian religion can be traced to the people's observation of the environment. Fundamental was the love of sunlight, the solar cycle and the comfort brought by the regular rhythms of nature, and the agricultural cycle surrounding the rise and fall of the Nile. Egyptian theology attempted, above all else, to explain these cosmic phenomena, incomprehensible to humans, by means of a series of understandable metaphors based on natural cycles and understandable experiences.[30]

For an ordinary Egyptian living during the Old Kingdom, these beliefs made perfect sense. They explained the unexplainable world and gave order to the chaos of life.

Gods and Goddesses

During the Old Kingdom the beliefs solidified into one all-encompassing religion. Because there were so many deities during the early predynastic days of the Egyptian civilization, Egyptians worshiped hundreds of gods and goddesses by the time of the Old Kingdom. Even individual nomes often had unique gods known only to that region.

This all-encompassing religion was a curious mix of two concepts: the Deities were all powerful, but they also were humanlike. The gods controlled the world, but they had to be accessible to the common citizen. Gods were born, they married, gave birth, ate, drank,

This wall painting depicts Hathor (right), the goddess of love and dance, shown here with the god Anubis (left) and King Tutankhamen.

This artwork depicts "The Tribunal of the Dead," a ceremony in which a dead person's heart is weighed against a feather to determine if he or she will proceed to the afterlife.

hunted, and fought in battle. They also had human emotions. Historians explain this idea by saying that, "to a great extent, gods were patterned after humans—they were born, some died [and were reborn], and they fought amongst themselves. Yet as much as the gods' behavior resembled human behavior, they were immortal and always superior to humans."[31] Because of this belief, the Egyptians associated their gods—the controllers of the universe—with ordinary existence.

Gods Associated with Animals

A peculiar aspect of Egyptian religion is that most gods and goddesses were depicted as part animal, part human. Hathor, the goddess of love and dance, for example, was usually shown as a woman with a cow's head or a woman wearing a horned headdress. Horus, the hawk god, was shown with the head of a bird and the body of a man. Historians attempt to explain this complicated idea by noting that

> further complicating our understanding of the early gods is the fact that a single deity could be represented in human form, in zoomorphic [animal] form or in a mixed animal-human form. . . . It is unlikely that the gods were derived from totemic [symbolic] animals. . . . Rather, animal forms were probably used to suggest metaphorically something about the characteristics of the god.[32]

No one is sure why the Egyptian gods were so closely linked with animals. Some historians think that the Egyptians depicted gods and goddesses with the heads of animals so that people could tell the various gods apart. For an illiterate population, this would be an easy way to distinguish one god from another. Other scholars believe that the Egyptians linked their gods and animals because of their reverence for the natural world and the balance of the universe. Despite all of these theories, it is clear that the animal-god connection in ancient Egypt was very important.

Maat and the Human Spirit

Some deities, however, were not associated with animals at all. Maat, one of the most important figures in Egyptian religion, for

The Egyptian Book of the Dead *contains this illustration of Anubis supporting a mummy during "The Opening of the Mouth" ceremony.*

example, took on only a human form. Maat was a goddess, and she represented truth and the balance of the universe. According to historian Christine El Mahdy,

> A deity recognized by all Egyptians was Maat, a goddess shown as a woman with a standing feather on her head, and who represented all that was the opposite of chaos. If Maat were satisfied, she would bring equilibrium and balance to daily life. And when the heart of the deceased was judged by the gods, it was weighed against the feather of truth, symbolizing the goddess Maat.[33]

But Maat was not only a goddess. She was also a state of mind, a concept somewhat like honor, justice, or honesty. For an ordinary Egyptian, *maat* meant working hard and being honest, treating people fairly and justly. Good *maat* gave a sense of order and linked all aspects of daily behavior and thought with the cosmos and the universe. As historians Brewer and Teeter explain,

> This sense of order . . . intertwined all aspects of correct daily behavior and thought with cosmic order and harmony. Individuals were personally responsible for the maintenance of the universal order. If one transgressed against the forces of that order, chaos—a state antithetical to everything the Egyptians knew and valued—would ensue and in this frightening realm [the Egyptians believed that] the sun would not rise, the Nile would not flood, crops would not grow, and children would abandon their elderly parents.[34]

Maat had to be maintained in the larger world as well, and that was the responsibility of the king. He did this through his relationship with the deities and by the rituals and other religious actions that the priests performed in his name every day.

The importance of not disrupting the *maat* can be seen in the Egyptian *Book of the Dead,* a text that usually appeared in coffins and tombs. It was believed that the deceased read this at his or her judgment before the gods. One passage reads, in part, "I have not done wrong; I have not slain people; I was not sullen; I have not caused anyone to weep; I have not had intercourse with a married woman."[35]

After this speech, the dead person's heart would be weighed against the feather of Maat. If the two balanced, then the deceased was allowed to pass into the afterlife. If the heart were heavy with wrongdoings, the person's soul would be devoured by a horrible god-monster. If the soul were devoured, Egyptians believed, it would return to the world as an evil spirit.

Death and the Afterlife

To many scholars, the Egyptians seemed preoccupied with death, and the preponderance of death imagery in Egyptian art and religion does imply that the Egyptians were obsessed with death. Although it is true that many of their most prominent gods were associated with death and afterlife rituals, the Egyptian civilization rejoiced in life and the living, and the funerary beliefs that arose in the Old Kingdom were a direct attempt to bring order and control to the most fearful aspect of life: death. Death was frightening and unwelcomed.

This wall painting depicts Tutankhamen, center, and his ka *standing before the god Osiris (left).*

The biography of one Egyptian, Taimehotep, includes a passage that clearly shows how the Egyptians viewed death:

> As for death "Come" is its name,
>
> All those that he calls to him come to him immediately;
>
> Their hearts afraid through dread of him.
>
> He snatches the son from his mother
>
> Frightened, they all plead before him,
>
> But he does not listen to them.[36]

The Egyptians used their religion to make sense of the life cycle and to make death less terrifying.

Although the Egyptians feared death, they also respected it. Through their religious beliefs, they sought to transform the end of life into something they could understand and be less frightened about. As a result, they created beliefs and rituals that reinforced the idea that death was not an end but a transition from one world to another that was an exact image of the first.

Ka, Ba, and *Akh*

Many of these ideas surrounded the different aspects of what modern people today think of as the human soul. The Egyptians believed that the human soul was made up of three different parts: the *ka*, the *ba*, and the *akh*.

The *ka* represented a person's life energy. According to historian El Mahdy,

> An infant, it was believed, was placed in its mother's womb after being created

> on a potter's wheel by the ram-headed god Khnum. But as Khnum formed the body he also fashioned a spiritual copy, resembling the body in every way, with all its needs, desires, and expectations. This was the ka, ghostly in appearance and stored in the heart.[37]

Ka was present throughout a person's life and was depicted on tombs and in other Egyptian art as an exact physical double of a person, with one addition—a special hieroglyph of two upraised arms on the figure's head. Egyptologist James Henry Breasted describes this belief: "[Egyptians] believed that the body was animated by a vital force, which was a counterpart of the body, which came into the world with it, passed through life in its company, and accompanied it to the next world. It was called a 'ka,' and it is often spoken of in modern treatises [accounts] as a 'double.'"[38]

When a person died, the *ka* separated from the body but remained on Earth in spiritual form. Although this spirit was not a physical being, it still needed food and drink just like a living human. Egyptians believed that the *ka* could enter a statue of a person who had died and use the offerings made to the statue. As a result, hundreds of funerary inscriptions include lists of the items the *ka* needed, such as "a thousand of bread, a thousand of beer, oxen, and fowl for the ka of the deceased."[39]

Another division of the soul was called the *ba*. The person's *ba* was not a physical part of the body, but was the element that made a person unique, similar to an individual's personality. Depicted as a bird with a human head, it represented the part of the deceased that was able to communicate between the land of the living and the afterlife. Historians Brewer and Teeter explain one way in which the *ba* could communicate with the people on Earth: "In some texts, the chirping of birds is equated with the chatter of the dead, serving as a reminder to those still alive of the eternal presence of the souls of the departed."[40]

The *ba* was a calm, comforting presence, and many texts refer to it as something to be honored and cherished. Egyptians believed that the *ba* stayed with the mummy in the dark, silent tombs at night as a comfort. In one famous text called the *Papyrus Anastasi I*, written during the Nineteenth Dynasty (approximately 1320–1200 B.C.), a scribe named Hori wrote this blessing:

> May you observe the rays of the sun and be satiated thereby. May you spend your lifetime in happiness with your gods pleased with you without displaying anger. May your reward be received after old age. . . . May you enter your tomb of the necropolis and associate with the excellent Bas. May you be judged among them and be declared righteous.[41]

The third part of the soul was called the *akh*. The *akh* was the power and spirit of the deceased. The *akh* was depicted in tomb art and paintings as the person him- or herself, with no special hieroglyphs or symbols. Egyptians believed that a person's spirit, in the form of the *akh*, could mingle with the gods.

The thought that a person would eventually live with the gods was a vital part of the death process. It reinforced the idea of a stable, predictable world and gave Egyptians something to which to look forward. In the ancient Egyptian text *Dialogue of a Man with*

His Soul, a man accepts his impending death and proceeds to rejoice in it as his entry into paradise:

> Death is to me today like a sick man's recovery,
>
> like going outside after confinement.
>
> Death is to me today like the scent of myrrh,
>
> like sitting under a sail on a windy day.
>
> Death is to me today like a well-trodden path,
>
> like a man's coming home from an expedition.
>
> Death is to me today like the opening of the sky,
>
> like a man's grasping what he did not know.
>
> Death is to me today like a man's longing to see home,
>
> having spent many years abroad.[42]

By the end of the Old Kingdom, most of the foundations of Egyptian society had been laid. In the years that followed, the first six dynasties were remembered as the golden age of Egypt. The kings who ruled during this time, including Djoser, Khufu, and others, became part of myths and legends. Long after the Old Kingdom had passed into history, Egyptians sought to recreate some of the splendor and glory of that time. For them, as for us today, the golden age represented the best they had ever been.

Chapter Four

The Flowering of Egypt: The Middle Kingdom

As the Old Kingdom came to an end, Egypt was a land torn apart by a variety of factors, including a climate change that may have affected the Nile and the crops. These changes threw Egypt's ordered, predictable world into uncertainty. There were a series of kings during this time, and each had a relatively short reign, suggesting political instability, which undoubtedly led to unrest. Although the kings continued to build temples, they did not construct grand pyramids. Artwork and architecture, although still impressive, lost much of its splendor.

As a result of the political unrest, the once proud Egypt splintered into dozens of independent states. The king dealt with *nomarches* and priests wielding political influence, a situation that in turn began to change the role of the king from an all-powerful god to a godlike being. This subtle shift would affect the entire scope of Egyptian society during the next era, the Middle Kingdom, which lasted roughly from 2040 to 1782 B.C.

This slow, gradual change could not have been seen by the ordinary Egyptian. It took place over hundreds of years, and there was no single, great upheaval in the society. Indeed, most Egyptians of the time would insist that little had changed. However, modern scholars who look back on the scope of Egyptian history can clearly see that Egyptian society was moving in new directions—toward the rise of the common individual.

King Nebhetepre Montuhotpe II and the Eleventh Dynasty

At the beginning of the Middle Kingdom, a strong king named Nebhetepre Montuhotpe II finally settled the unrest and reunified Egypt. Scholars know little about how he accomplished this, but it is certain that he reunified Egypt and began the Eleventh Dynasty (approximately 2133–1991 B.C.) of Egyptian rulers. He is one of the greatest Egyptian kings, and his rule ushered in an era when art, literature, and culture thrived and grew. Historian Michael Rice paints a clear picture of the king when he says,

> Nebhetepre Montuhotpe II was one of the greatest of Egypt's kings, confident, determined, clear of purpose and swift in action. He reigned long, for more than fifty years; he was thus

> able to direct the reunification of the Valley and to see it very largely achieved in his lifetime. . . . He proclaimed himself the Horus Sematowy, "the Uniter of the Two Lands."[43]

The dynasty that began with Nebhetepre Montuhotpe's rule marked the beginning of the Middle Kingdom. The kings of the Eleventh Dynasty reestablished trade with foreign countries, repaired public structures, began irrigation projects, and encouraged the writing of texts. This new prosperity gave Egyptians a welcome respite from the black days that had come before. The world was once again fresh and full of hope. A strong, stable king was once again on the throne. The Nile seemed to be settling down to its regular pattern of flooding. The gods seemed happy with the Egyptian people, finally. As a result, the Egyptians were able to focus on artistic and cultural achievement in ways that had never before been seen.

The all-encompassing power of a god-king, however, never returned. Historians suspect that this was partly due to the fact that towns and villages became accustomed to their independence during the years of unrest. Local politicians had more power, and they wanted to keep it. Only well into the Middle Kingdom era did a king, Senusret III, finally break the local governors and return the monarchy to its previous power. But by that time, the idea of the king as an omnipotent god was gone for good.

The Rise of the Individual

The dawning of the Middle Kingdom ushered in a new concept in Egyptian society: the importance of the individual. Prior to this time, the art, architecture, and sculpture focused primarily on the king and his life on

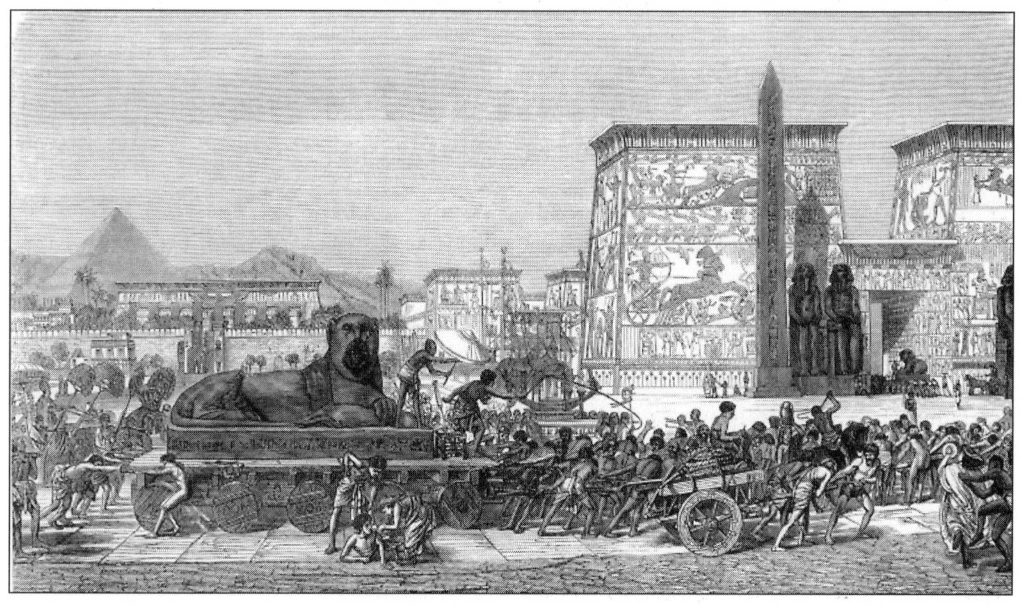

During the Eleventh Dynasty, Egyptian kings oversaw the reparation of public structures, building of irrigation projects, and flourishing of written texts.

Earth and with the gods. This suggests that only the king, and perhaps some high officials, had access to an afterlife. During the Middle Kingdom, however, artwork began to depict other Egyptians, pointing to the rise in a belief that more people could expect to enjoy the fruits of the afterlife. As Rice explains, "In the Middle Kingdom, this anonymous mass begins to separate and to take on individual identities. Lesser officials, priests in the lower ranks of the temple administrations and soldiers are named, as are the stewards of estates and the upper servants of the magnates [high-ranking people]."[44]

Although it is unclear when or how this belief arose, historians offer many suggestions. Perhaps it evolved as a result of the uncertainty of past times, when the world was in chaos and people needed to believe they would someday be in a better place. Political unrest also may have compelled the people to turn to religion as a place of stability and order. Art historian Cyril Aldred subscribes to this theory. He explains that "the traumatic collapse of the Old Kingdom . . . turned men's minds to the promise of eternal life [in the afterlife] by the side of a resurrected god. The . . . erection of a stela or votive statuette [a type of statue that had heiroglyphs on it] . . . became of more importance for many Egyptians than burial near their lord."[45]

This Sphinx, one piece of art created during the Middle Kingdom, reached six feet high.

Egyptian Artists

Regardless of the origins of this shift, by the Middle Kingdom it is clear that most ordinary Egyptians believed that they, like the king, had a right to walk with the gods in the afterlife. Because more people had access to the afterlife, it became even more important for them to have elaborate tombs in which they could rest after death. Artisans and craftspeople who created the tomb paintings, sculpture, and funerary objects became increasingly important to society. As a result, their art flourished and became a hallmark of this era of Egyptian civilization. As historians Douglas Brewer and Emily Teeter describe, "[Middle Kingdom] gold and jewelry, much of which is inlaid with colored stone, exhibits a refinement of design and technique that was never surpassed."[46]

Clearly, the ancient Egyptian artists of the Middle Kingdom were highly skilled. The breathtaking tomb paintings, sculpture, and architecture that still remain show a culture that revered and respected beauty.

Paintings and tomb reliefs were not simply decorations, however. They were created to represent events and people in a timeless world they hoped would never change. To the Egyptian, art was not a means of individual expression. Instead, images created with paint and stone depicted the world as the Egyptians believed it existed. For example, kings commissioned paintings of themselves in victory because they believed they would be victorious in battle. For the Egyptians, and especially the people of the Middle Kingdom, it was vital that they continue to control their world through architecture, art, and literature. The Middle Kingdom artisans worked steadily toward this goal.

Architecture in the Middle Kingdom

The Middle Kingdom was a time of great artistic achievement in all areas, but it was in architecture that the Egyptians shone. During the dark days before the rise of the Middle Kingdom era, the people longed to return to the glory of the Old Kingdom. They considered that time to be their golden age, when powerful kings built glorious structures such as grand temples and majestic pyramids. When the political unrest settled during the Middle Kingdom, the people—and the kings—finally had an opportunity to focus their attention on rebuilding Egypt. Architects and artisans looked to the models of Old Kingdom architecture for inspiration. However, they did not want to merely copy the Old Kingdom styles, they wanted to build even more wonderful structures. According to historian Rice, they achieved their goals: "Such buildings as survive [from the Middle Kingdom] are very beautiful, often of a splendidly balanced austerity which recalled, but does not emulate, the best of the Old Kingdom architecture."[47]

Great Structures of the Middle Kingdom

One of the most breathtaking surviving Middle Kingdom buildings is the Senusret Kiosk in modern-day Karnak. Karnak is the site of one of the most majestic temple complexes in Egypt. It was built over the course of many years, and king after king added to it until it became an enormous structure that today covers about five acres of land. This kiosk is part of the oldest section of Karnak, and it was used as a way station, or stopping place, for priests carrying statues of the god from place to place during religious celebrations, parades, and processions. The kiosk is built of golden polished limestone and is covered with elaborate carvings of kings and gods. Historian Christine Hobson describes the kiosk: "The reliefs on the walls of this small building are outstanding, with some of the finest detail to be seen on any relief work in Egypt."[48]

Another great example of Middle Kingdom architecture, also found near Karnak, is the funerary monument of Nebhetepre Montuhotpe II. Its richness and originality were unparalleled. The complex was built against a rock cliff, three levels high and surrounded by the cool shade of trees. A great court graced the entrance of the complex, and ramps led from the court to the upper levels. A small pyramid rose at the top of the complex, but it was only for show. The true tomb was carved into the cliff. The courtyard was lined with standing and seated figures that watched majestically over all who passed by.

Another impressive Middle Kingdom structure was the huge tomb complex of the Middle Kingdom king Amenemhet III. Although little of the tomb now remains, this immense

THE EVOLUTION OF EGYPTIAN ARCHITECTURE

The earliest Egyptian architecture was little more than elaborate tents, which consisted of woven reed mats stretched between wooden poles. These simple structures included elements that would eventually become common characteristics of grand Egyptian buildings. For example, mats were gathered and tied at the corners, making a rounded edge. As a decorative element in stone, these rounded corners were called torus molding. Sometimes the edges of the mats became frayed and hung over the top of the structure. This eventually became an architectural element called a cavetto cornice, which was a decorative edging carved to look like long ridges that ran along the top of a building.

Most information about Egyptian architecture comes from the surviving temple ruins. The earliest temples were simple structures, built of mud brick, mats, thatch, and other lightweight materials. They included a sanctuary and a few small rooms. Even when temples began to be constructed from stone, they still retained some of the styles of the older tent structures. Historians Emily Teeter and Douglas Brewer explain this evolution in their book *Egypt and the Egyptians.*

> "Although stone, the Djoser temples [from the Old Kingdom] appear to have copied the design of the earlier perishable temples, suggesting that the walls of the early temples were mats stretched on poles and that the characteristic features of later architecture [torus molding and cavetto cornices] were established quite early."

Eventually temples became vast, majestic structures. These structures, now considered to be uniquely Egyptian, were designed and developed over thousands of years. The Egyptian civilization was one of the first societies to create its own style of buildings and architecture, and the buildings have lasted to delight and amaze people throughout history.

structure was so beautiful that it survived about 1,700 years until Greco-Roman times. Its mazelike passageways are thought to have given rise to the legends of the labyrinth. The Greek historian Herodotus, who visited Egypt in the fifth century, described the wonder of this great Middle Kingdom structure:

> The pyramids are astonishing structures. . . . But the labyrinth surpasses them all. . . . Inside, the building is of two stories and contains 3,000 rooms, of which half are underground and the other half above them. . . . It is hard to believe they are all the work

> of men. The baffling and winding corridors from room to room and courtyard to courtyard were an endless wonder to me. . . . The walls are covered with carved figures and each courtyard is faced with superb white marble, surrounded by a colonnade [a series of columns].[49]

Unfortunately, only a few Middle Kingdom era buildings have survived the ravages of time, but these structures show a fresh style and beauty that had never been seen in Egypt. This new style of architecture suggests that, for the first time, Egyptians were becoming more aware of themselves as part of the larger structure of Egyptian civilization. The care with which they created the structures, and the artwork that graced them, indicate that ordinary citizens were beginning to understand and appreciate their role in the larger world.

One of the few surviving structures of ancient Egypt, this hall of the Temple of Amun reflects a new style of architecture that developed during the Middle Kingdom.

Art of the Middle Kingdom

During the Middle Kingdom, art also achieved new levels of beauty and skill. During that time, ordinary citizens began to commission artworks for their own tombs. They wanted to depict their lives and their journey to the afterlife on their tombs and coffins. In doing so, they believed they could predict the kind of reception they would receive when they reached the lands of the gods. The artwork served to chronicle their lives of honesty and good *maat*, the long journey from death to the afterlife, the gods who would greet them, and the joy they would feel as they began their new existence in a strange, eternal world.

Sculpture

There were various kinds of tomb art, and sculpture was one of the more important ones. As more ordinary citizens clamored for tomb statuary, there arose two distinct kinds of sculpture: those made for royal tombs and those made for private citizens. Huge, elaborate statues of kings were created for the royal temples, pyramids, and royal tombs. Sculptures commissioned by private individuals were placed in tombs and burial chambers, and they tended to be less elaborate. But the two kinds of sculpture shared one important trait: They were created to ensure a person's happy existence in the afterlife. According to historian A. Rosalie David, "The main aim was to produce an idealized figure, free from physical defects, and according to a prescribed set of rules.

The patron was assured of eternal life by the simple device of adding his name to the statue, thus establishing the identification of the statue with him."[50]

Regardless of whether the person commissioning the statue were royal or ordinary, however, the style of the artwork maintained the same level of exquisite beauty for which the era was known. Middle Kingdom statuary was elegant and formal, and individual pieces show a new level of sophistication and skill from the carvers.

Although royal tomb art continued to depict the king in the traditional role of a god-like figure, during the Middle Kingdom, he was more often shown as an individual as well. Michael Rice explains this, saying, "Middle Kingdom statuary is immediately recognizable. It has a formality and solidity which are deeply impressive; it is also entirely human in scale, [even though] royal portraits still defer to the convention of the king as god."[51]

A specific kind of royal statuary that was widely used is that of sphinx carvings, and many of them reflect the importance of the individual likeness in Egyptian civilization. Kings of this time delighted in having their likenesses depicted on sphinxes, and many of

FRONTALISM

The most noticeable aspect of Egyptian painting and relief is in the way that the human figure is depicted. Regardless of what time in Egypt's history a painting or relief was created, the images are almost always shown in profile and the body is turned in such a way as to be seen from the front. This style, called frontalism, pervades Egyptian art. Every figure stands or sits in a stiff and formal manner. The eyes are drawn in full, and most faces show a calm, serene expression.

But the stiff, formal poses of the figures do not mean that the artists were unskilled or inexperienced. Rather, it reflects their religious beliefs and attitudes toward death and dying. To the Egyptians, who strove for organization and control, artwork had a real power to affect the world. It was vital that art depicted not what really existed but what was believed to exist.

Egyptian painters developed a unique artistic style called frontalism (shown here).

As art evolved during the Middle Kingdom era, paintings began to depict the daily lives of ordinary Egyptians.

these statues still survive. These sphinxes are really portraits, which show the Middle Kingdom kings as strong, powerful rulers. However, a hint to the changes in the idea of the king as an individual can be seen in the faces of some royal sphinx carvings. Their broad, serene faces are carved with the small, care-worn details that give them a human quality: wrinkles beneath the eyes, drawn mouths, stern expressions. The attention to reality in these sculptures is a mark of Middle Kingdom artistry, but it also gives the kings an air of mortality—perhaps a subtle reflection of the change in the religious beliefs of the time.

Paintings and Reliefs

Wall paintings and reliefs were no less important, and Middle Kingdom artisans excelled in creating the lifelike images that filled temple walls. The actual techniques of painting and wall relief did not change much during the Middle Kingdom, suggesting that artisans did not enjoy the kinds of innovations the sculptors seemed to embrace. However, the distinction of Middle Kingdom art is that, more and more, the lives of ordinary citizens became the subject of tomb paintings. Portraits became popular, and portrait artists eclipsed their predecessors in skill and technique.

The great king Senusret III commissioned some of the most remarkable portraits of the era, some of which are still around today. They show the king as young and old, depicting the transition from a carefree young man to a worried, care-worn king. The artists clearly captured a man with a weary, dejected expression, showing that a king-god could also have mortal worries.

The king, however, was not the only subject of the artist's brush in the Middle Kingdom. The time is rich with portraits of lesser people as well—mainly officials and priests—which show their personality and individuality. During the Middle Kingdom, tomb scenes that once might have depicted religious stories or deities began to represent individuals. Scenes from everyday life also began to appear during this time. Historian Cyril Aldred describes these new innovations:

> The paintings . . . give vivid pictures of everyday life in all its bustle, Middle Kingdom versions of most of the scenes that decorate Old Kingdom mastabas, with some new introductions of dress, pose, and accoutrements. Scenes of wrestling, battle and siege warfare [for example] appear commonly, whereas they are very rare in the Old Kingdom.[52]

Craftsmen such as jewelers (depicted at work in this mural painting) created exquisite and beautiful products.

The Minor Arts

The high arts of painting and sculpture were not the only ones to enjoy a new resurgence during the Middle Kingdom. The lesser arts and crafts also brought beauty and richness into the lives of ordinary Egyptians, and the objects that artisans created are some of the most exquisite examples of Middle Kingdom art that survive. The skilled laborers who created those pieces were the backbone of the Egyptian civilization, and it was these highly trained people who contributed their skills and their talents to the beauty that was the Middle Kingdom. Craftsmen such as jewelers, weavers, and perfumers supplied specific goods to Egyptians. Many of these people excelled in their crafts, and their work remains some of the most exquisite ancient Egypt had to offer.

Most craftspeople worked in workshops associated with the king or with a particular temple. These workshops produced a variety of objects, including vessels, textiles, furniture, and jewelry, and most of the objects made in these workshops were used in temple rituals and in the funerary caches of the deceased. As a result, much of their work has survived the ages. Their works, like those of the sculptors and artists, defined the new flowering of the Middle Kingdom with a fresh attention to detail and creative energy. As historian Rice says, "The minor arts flourished in the Middle Kingdom. Some of the finest and most resplendent jewelry made in Egypt has been recovered from burials of Middle

Kingdom princesses, works of great beauty and exceptional craftsmanship."[53]

These artworks are set apart mainly by the skill of the craftspeople who created them. They chose beautiful materials such as precious beads and gold, and they had a great deal of knowledge about how to craft such materials into objects.

One example of this can be found in a set of black stone cups made during this time. The cups are very simple, but the carefully polished stone shines. They are decorated with a single fine gold line around their rims, giving them a quiet elegance. Cups such as these—ordinary objects elevated to the status of beautiful artwork—symbolize the new artistic awakening of the Middle Kingdom and of the Egyptians' growing awareness of the beauty of everyday life and the individual's importance in the larger world.

Anonymous Artists

Although the artists of the Middle Kingdom were more skilled than any others who proceeded them, little is known about the individuals who created the sculptures, paintings, and objects of the time. Egyptian artisans were considered to be no more than laborers providing needed services. Their art was never intended to be seen after it was complete. Historian David explains:

> The decoration of a tomb was a united effort, in which several artists or relief-sculptors would work together under the general guidance of the Master. Each man was responsible for a part of the work, and did not seek individual recognition. Indeed, the art is anonymous, except in a few instances. It was never intended that scholars and tourists [who have visited the monuments from the Roman period onward] should enter the sacred temples and tombs, gaze upon the artist's work and pass judgment upon its aesthetic merits.[54]

A few artists, however, did try to make themselves known. A tomb inscription, for example, reveals the pride of workmanship that one Middle Kingdom artisan had. It reads, "I was an artist skilled in my art, preeminent in my learning. . . . I knew [how to represent] the movements of the image of a man and the carriage of a woman. . . . The posing of the arm to bring the hippopotamus low and the movements of the runner."[55] The pride that this man had in his work was probably shared by many other Egyptian artisans.

Several artists worked together to decorate a tomb. Their work included wall paintings such as this one.

"TALE OF THE ELOQUENT PEASANT"

This story, one of the masterpieces of Middle Kingdom literature, was most likely written sometime during the Twelfth Dynasty. In the story, the peasant first pleads with an official for the return of his stolen donkeys. The official pretends to ignore the peasant just so that he can continue hearing the poor man's beautiful words. Eventually the official takes the peasant to the king, who delights in the peasant's eloquence as well. Throughout the story, people are amazed that such a poor, common man can speak with such beauty and emotion.

In this section of the story, reprinted in the book *Voices from Ancient Egypt* by R. B. Parkinson, the peasant criticizes an official, the high steward, for his greed and wealth, then accuses him of helping the thief who stole the donkeys.

"And this peasant came to appeal to him [the High Steward] an eighth time, saying,

'High Steward, my lord!

One falls for greed far.

The selfish one is free from success; his success belongs to failure.

You are selfish—it is not for you; you steal—it is no good for you, you who should have made a man attend to his good deed truly!

For it is the case that your portion is in your house, and your belly full, while the corn measure brims over and overflows,

so that its excess perishes on the ground.

Siezer of the robbed, taker!

The officials who were appointed to outlaw evil,

they are now a shelter for the predator,

those officials who were appointed to outlaw falsehood.

But your fearfulness does not make me appeal to you; you do not perceive my heart.'"

It is likely that they well understood how their talents contributed to the glory of the Egyptian civilization.

Literature

It was not only artisans who left their mark on Egyptian culture. Writers and scholars also displayed tremendous talents, and literature and storytelling reached a climax during the Middle Kingdom, specifically the Twelfth Dynasty (approximately 1991–1786 B.C.). Before this time, written works generally consisted of prayers and texts for the king, and most of them were religious-oriented legends and mythologies. As the Middle Kingdom era blossomed, people began to write secular, or nonreligious, tales and poetry that celebrated the individual and the joys of life. This shift, like the shift in other forms of art, represented a new concept in Egyptian society. Whereas before only gods and nobility were worthy of songs and poems, Egyptian writing now focused more on ordinary people and their exploits.

Most of the stories that survive from the Egyptian civilization were written during this era. At the time, they were so well loved that they became instant classics passed down from generation to generation. As historian George Stendorff explains, "The writings of this period were prized by the Egyptians as gems and constantly copied as 'classics' in the schools for scribes. It is for this reason that they have been preserved—many of them in more than one manuscript."[56]

Stories of the Middle Kingdom

One of these classics, called "The Story of Sinuhe," is about a palace official who flees Egypt after the death of the king and ultimately becomes a rich man in Syria. It is a classic rags-to-riches tale, and the main character of the story is an ordinary person, someone with whom other Egyptians could identify. Egyptologist James Henry Breasted describes the popularity and importance of this story:

> The unfortunate noble, Sinuhe, who fled into Syria on the death of [the king], returned to Egypt in his old age, and the story of his flight, of his life and adventures in Asia became a favorite tale, which attained such popularity that it was even written on sherds and flags of stone to be placed in the tomb for the entertainment of the dead in the hereafter.[57]

Another famous Middle Kingdom story, "The Tale of the Eloquent Peasant," is about a man who pleads so eloquently for the return of his stolen donkeys that he is brought before the king. This story also has an ordinary person as its main character. This time, however, the hero is a lowly peasant, not a rich official. Although he is a poor man, the peasant proves to be intelligent and clever as he deals with the Egyptian bureaucracy—illustrating the idea that the individual has an important role in Egyptian society. This story, says Breasted,

> was composed solely in order to place in the mouth of a marvelous peasant a series of speeches in which he pleads his case against an official who had wronged him, with such eloquence that he is at last brought into the presence of the Pharaoh himself, that the monarch may enjoy the beauty of the honeyed rhetoric which flows from his lips.[58]

This new attention to everyday life and the ordinary citizen in literature was just another aspect of the new importance of the individual in Middle Kingdom life. For the first time, common people were considered important and interesting. This era ushered in a new respect for the common man and for the simple details of everyday life. The new emphasis on the individual carried over into daily life and enabled citizens to fill their tombs with beautiful objects created by artisans who excelled in talent and skill. During the Middle Kingdom, art became important to everyone in Egyptian society, and it resulted in a flowering of beauty and culture that helped ancient Egypt, and its residents, thrive and prosper.

Chapter Five

The Last Great Age: The New Kingdom

To the common Egyptian men and women who walked the wide avenues of the great Egyptian cities in the last years before the dawn of the New Kingdom era, which lasted from 1570–1069 B.C., the world looked bleak. For two hundred years, between the end of the Middle Kingdom and the beginning of the New Kingdom, invasion and the horror of foreign rulers who lorded over Egypt had completely changed the Egyptians' way of thinking about their world. The all-powerful Egyptian kings, once considered to be gods, were proven fallible. The world had plunged into political chaos that affected everything they believed and all they had achieved. It was a bitter blow to realize that Egypt was no longer the most powerful country in the universe.

By the end of the Middle Kingdom, a series of weak kings made the throne vulnerable, and *nomarches*, priests, and other high officials rose against each other in a fight for the throne. One usurper would achieve the kingship, only to be defeated by another. As they squabbled, the economy crumbled. Irrigation projects and agricultural administration were ignored, and goods such as wheat and flax, which provided the basis of the economy, fell in short supply. The time was ripe for foreign invasion, and outsiders wasted no time in claiming the grand, rich Egyptian empire as their own.

The Hyksos Invasion

About 1675 B.C. a foreign people called the Hyksos poured into Egypt, overwhelmed the land, and took the throne without a battle. For the next two hundred years Egypt would chafe under Hyksos rulers who pillaged the land and destroyed much of the grandeur of Egypt. One early Egyptian document relates this horrible chain of events:

> I know not why, that God was displeased with us, and there came unexpectedly men of ignoble [common] birth out of the eastern parts, who had boldness enough to make an expedition into our country, and easily subdued it by force without a battle. And when they had got our rulers under their power, they afterward savagely burnt down our cities and demolished the temples of the gods, and used all the inhabitants in a most hostile manner, for they slew some and led the children and wives of others into slavery.[59]

Finally, in about 1546 B.C., a powerful Egyptian warrior by the name of Ahmose managed to unify Egypt and drive the Hyksos from the land. Historian A. Rosalie David describes the years of bloody warfare that finally resulted in Egyptian victory against the Hyksos:

> The princes of Thebes [a large Egyptian city] expelled the Hyksos from Egypt. Conflict began between the Hyksos ruler, Apophis, and Seqenenre of Thebes. The body of the latter, which we [modern researchers] still possess today, indicates by its terrible head wounds that the Thebian died in battle. His son, Kamose, continued the fight. . . . Apophis was driven from Middle Egypt. . . . The younger brother of Kamose, Ahmose, dealt the final blow. Having driven the Hyksos out of Egypt, [Ahmose] pursued them into Palestine, where he eliminated the danger in a series of campaigns. He then invaded the region of Kush, to the south of Egypt, which had allied with and supported the Hyksos. After a decade of fighting the supremacy of Egypt was assured. King Ahmose I inaugurated the New Kingdom and the Empire.[60]

Ahmose became the first king of the New Kingdom, and he had his work cut out for him. As one Egyptian document lamented, the king's job included "restoring that which lay in ruins; in building up that which was unfinished; and, since the Asiatics had been in Avaris in the Northland, in overthrowing that which had been done while they ruled in ignorance of Re."[61]

The land was in ruins, and its people were demoralized and fearful. The fields were in disarray. The well-oiled bureaucratic machine that had once run the government so smoothly was cracked. Priests and temple officials had their own political agendas to achieve power and wealth. Slowly, with great effort, King Ahmose and his successors lifted Egypt up once again and brought the world to a pinnacle of glory and achievement that was the New Kingdom—the last hallmark of Egyptian civilization.

Warfare

Egypt and the kings who ruled during the New Kingdom would never again be complacent in the idea that Egypt was the center of the universe or that the Egyptian king was a god. Experience had shown them that they

Mummy case of King Ahmose I.

were but one country in a vast world filled with other powerful rulers and armies. As historian Aldred relates,

> The Hyksos invasions had destroyed for ever the Egyptians' former belief in their uniqueness and superiority. The more intimate contacts that were now established with the high civilizations of Western Asia and the Aegean world brought home to them that their pharaoh, traditionally the incarnation of the god who had created their universe . . . in practice shared his sovereignty with brother monarchs in other lands.[62]

During the New Kingdom, Egypt, for the first time, became a military state. The king became a war hero, and the Egyptian armies flourished as they began their own invasions outside Egypt's borders. According to Aldred,

> The triumph of Ahmose on the field of battle introduced a new concept of the pharaoh as national hero, a personification of Egypt itself, and the leader of a military machine. . . . The pharaoh was now regarded as the incarnation of some warrior-god, Baal or Seth or Mentu, at the head of a caste of professional military leaders, accomplished in athletic sports and the management of horses, besides all the skills of a new mobile warfare.[63]

Before the New Kingdom, Egypt had no standing army because there was no real need for one. Agriculture and running the bureaucracy had always been far more important than warfare, not to mention the fact that there were few foes to fight. Although Egypt had always employed a group of professional soldiers and palace guards, troops were drawn from the general population whenever warfare threatened the country.

However, during the New Kingdom, a well-trained army became a necessity. The long wars against the Hyksos had created a strong, experienced Egyptian army that was the king's to use at will. After the defeat of the Hyksos, not only did the army serve to defend Egypt against hostile invaders, but it also served as an invader itself, overpowering smaller, weaker countries to exploit their riches and wealth. As Egyptologist James Breasted explains, "Having thoroughly learned war and having perceived the enormous wealth to be gained by it in Asia, the whole land [of Egypt] was roused and stirred with a lust of conquest, which was not quenched for several centuries."[64]

Egyptian Soldiers

A new career opened up for the average Egyptian: that of soldier. Being an Egyptian solider was a respected profession, and the wealth and prestige that came with being in the Egyptian army was a powerful incentive for young men to join. According to historian David,

> It was possible to gain rapid promotion and considerable riches in the service, and veterans were often given lands, gold decorations and war captives as domestic servants. . . . The army offered the uneducated man a means of acquiring some wealth, and foreigners who entered the service gained their freedom. An additional incentive was provided by the regulation which en-

THE MILITARY LIFE

The military life was an exciting prospect for young Egyptian boys, but the life of a soldier was not as glamorous as some thought it to be. In *The Literature of the Ancient Egyptians*, author Adolph Erman quotes an Egyptian school text that encourages students to choose the life of a scribe over the life of a soldier.

"Come, let me tell you how the soldier lives . . . while yet a child to be shut up in the barracks. He receives a burning blow on his body, a ruinous blow on his eye, a blow that knocks him down on his eyebrow, and his pate is cleft with a wound. . . . Let me tell you how he goes to Syria and marches up the mountains. His bread and water are borne upon his shoulder like the load of an ass; the joints of his back are bowed. His drink is stinking water. . . . When he reaches the enemy, he is like a trapped bird, and he has no strength in his limbs. If he comes home to Egypt, he . . . becomes bedridden. His clothes are stolen and his servants have run away. . . . Turn away from the thought that the soldier is better off than the scribe!"

This limestone relief depicts Egyptian soldiers; the life of a soldier seemed glamorous to young Egyptian boys, but the reality was quite different.

abled the sons of a regular soldier to inherit their father's land—the gift of the king—only if they followed in their father's career.[65]

People from all walks of life joined up. Those of the middle class and even sons of the king, who were once part of the royal nobility, now sought the excitement and adventure of

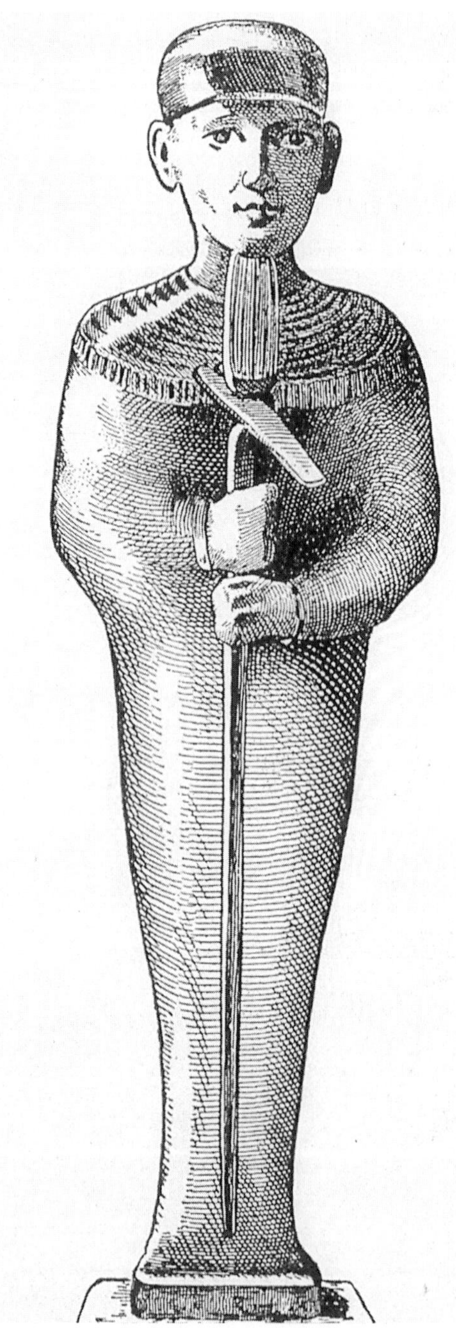

One of the subdivisions of the Egyptian army was named after the god of the Divine Spirit, Ptah (pictured).

military careers. Sons of nobles and high officials also saw the military life as an alternative to a dull bureaucratic career. One Egyptian wrote an autobiography that included his experiences with the Egyptian military, and he described some of the people who made up the division in which he was assigned:

> My majesty [the king] sent me at the head of this army, there being counts, royal seal-bearers, sole companions of the palace, chieftains and mayors of towns of Upper and Lower Egypt and chief district leaders, chief priests of Upper and Lower Egypt . . . at the head of the troops . . . from the villages and towns that they governed.[66]

The rising importance of the Egyptian military was a symbol of the great changes occurring in the country during that time. Egyptians were becoming more aware of the outside world and the dangers it held. There was a fresh sense of patriotism and a desire to defend their country and their way of life. People no longer relied on the king and their gods to protect them. This realization touched the core of everything the Egyptians once believed in and, as a result, eventually changed the way people viewed themselves, their beliefs, and their culture.

Military Divisions

The organization of the army, much like the organization of Egyptian society, was ordered and controlled. The Egyptian army was separated into two large divisions, one in Lower Egypt and another in Upper Egypt. These armies were further divided into four subdivisions, each named for a god: Amun, Ptah, Re, and Seth. Each of these larger divisions was subdivided into squadrons under captains and lower-ranking officers. There were also troops of mercenaries, which were foreign soldiers who fought with the Egyptians for a fee. The divisions and squadrons all had their own names and each carried some kind of banner or identifying symbol, such as a feather or a colored bit of cloth. These were tied to their spears and were raised high during the march.

Most Egyptians in the military were foot soldiers called infantrymen, and their weapons were simple but effective—bows, slings, spears, battle axes, and maces. All infantrymen wore light body armor made of padded fabric, and they carried round or oval shields covered with hide. Furthermore, the Egyptians' skill with the bow was so renowned that their reputation as a deadly force lasted for centuries.

A Powerful Weapon

As the armies of the New Kingdom grew stronger, they gained a new and powerful weapon. The Hyksos introduced horses and a new invention called the chariot into Egypt during their time in power, and by the beginning of the New Kingdom, Egyptian armies possessed a large number of chariots. Soon chariot makers were churning out hundreds of the lightweight, two-wheeled vehicles. Chariots

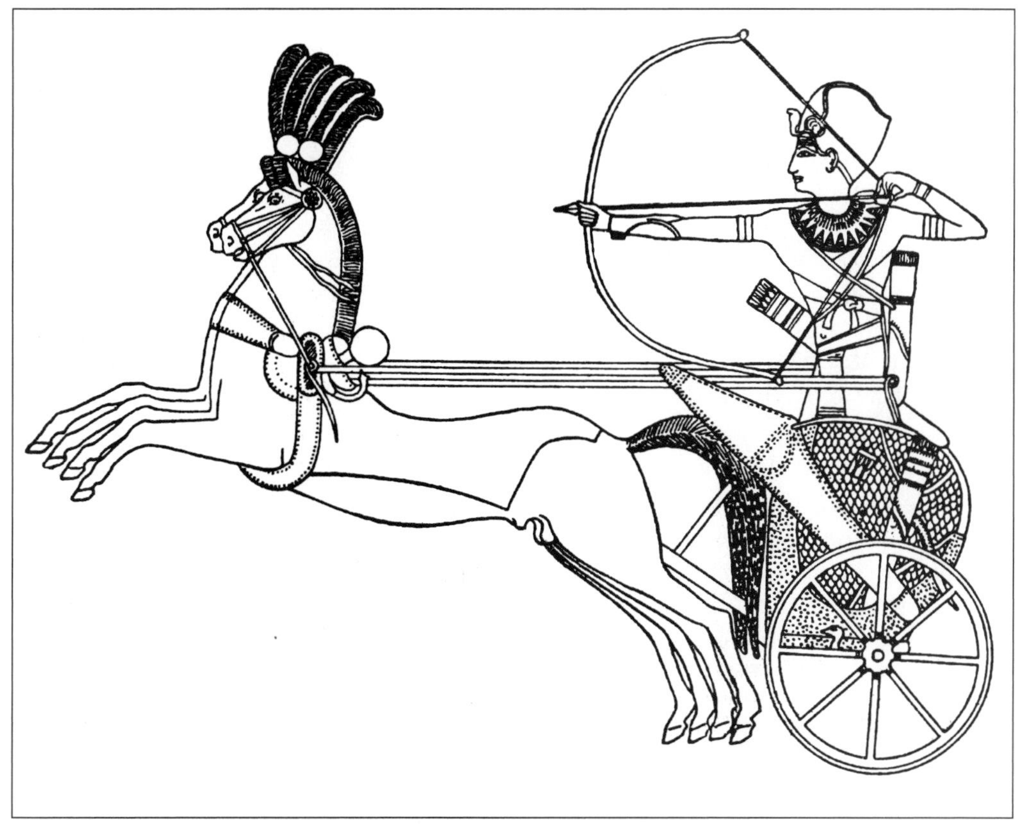

Horses and chariots, introduced by the Hyksos, revolutionized Egyptian warfare.

revolutionized Egyptian warfare because they enabled entire squadrons of soldiers to make lightning-fast attacks.

Chariot forces were usually divided into squadrons of twenty-five chariots apiece, and each chariot had two men inside—a driver and a soldier. The soldier was usually heavily armed with spears, bows, and a shield, but the driver was not armed and did not wear armor.

Historian Leonard Cottrell's book *Life Under the Pharaohs* includes one inscription that survived from the New Kingdom and describes both infantry and chariot forces. The number of men in the army hints at the vastness of the Egyptian forces. It reads, "The actual field army was organized into divisions, each of which was a complete army corps consisting of both chariotry and infantry and numbering about 5,000 men."[67]

For generations, the Egyptian army grew stronger and more powerful as the leaders of the New Kingdom rose in power as well. The New Kingdom era would be forever known as the time of the powerful Egyptian army.

Medicine and Magic in the New Kingdom

It was not only in military strength that the Egyptians of the New Kingdom excelled. The New Kingdom is also known as a time when scholarly learning gained headway within society, and one of the most important topics of study was medicine and the human body.

The Egyptians had studied medicine from the earliest days of their civilization. Egyptian records show that King Djoser of the First Dynasty was a respected physician who wrote about anatomy. Imhotep, the famous pyramid architect of the Old Kingdom, was also a physician. His reputation was so revered that he was later worshiped by the Greeks as a god of medicine.

Despite their reverence for doctors, medicine in ancient Egypt was not really a science. The Egyptians believed that illness was the work of the gods, and physicians were also considered to be priests. An Egyptian who got sick understood that it was most likely the act of a hostile spirit, disgruntled god, or deceased person holding a grudge from beyond the grave. Such people sought out the physician, who was usually affiliated with a local temple, and asked the gods and the healer to remove the evil that had inflicted their bodies. One historian explains: "At times of illness especially, the physician priests from the temple . . . would be called. The priest would consult the writings, and from the symptoms of the illness would declare whether or not he was able to treat the problem."[68]

If the physician determined that the illness had been brought upon the person by the gods as punishment for some wrongdoing or to end a life at the appropriate time, then he would not treat the patient. If the illness were found to have come from a demon who was using the body as a battlefield against the god, then the writings would assure the doctor that something could be done to treat the ailment. In that case, the physician would say incantations and give the patient potions and amulets to ward off the evil spirits. These beliefs were tied to the Egyptians' strong belief in the spirit world, *maat*, and the influences of the gods on the life of the mortal world. Because the Egyptians believed that illness sprang in large part from these mystical, mysterious influences, it was natural for them to believe that only magic could dispel the evil and cure the sickness. By the New Kingdom, the concepts of med-

EGYPTIAN PRESCRIPTION MEDICINE

Egyptian physicians were quite advanced for their time, and they were able to heal many common ailments. They usually kept detailed notes on papyrus, in which they described the medical problems of their patients and the treatment they used. Surviving texts on anatomy and physiology show a great deal of knowledge of the workings of the human body, its structure, and the job of the heart and blood vessels.

The physicians also kept detailed records of the medicines they used. Some of these prescriptions exist today, and they show treatment of many disorders and the use of a variety of substances, including plant, animal, and mineral materials. The droppings and urine of a number of animals, such as pelicans and hippopotamuses, were also widely used. Honey and milk were used to treat respiratory ailments and throat irritations. The Egyptians even practiced dentistry, and they filled cavities with a type of mineral cement. Eye disease was a big problem due to dust, flies, and poor hygiene, so many prescriptions existed to cure these problems.

It is unclear if any of their cures actually worked. Scholars, however, agree that the Egyptians were highly aware of the problems of the body and tried many remedies to relieve a sick and injured person's pain.

icine and magic were so closely entwined that they were inseparable.

Regardless of the Egyptians' reliance on magic in medicine, they also understood and used many medicines with real healing properties, including certain types of plants. Egyptian doctors, according to A. Rosalie David,

> knew how to use splints, bandages, and compresses. Certain tomb scenes show the application of splints around fractured bones, and the setting of a dislocated shoulder. They also made use of medicines and balms. Ointments were made up, using a basis of honey or fats, and applied externally to wounds and sores. For certain ailments special diets were suggested, such as honey, cream, and milk for chest and throat complaints.[69]

In the New Kingdom, and perhaps farther back in Egyptian history, physicians made a clear distinction between the illnesses and injuries that were known and understood and those whose origins were a mystery. For common ailments, such as injuries from falls or blows, there were straightforward medical treatments. For others, physicians used a combination of medicine and magic. This was due to the fact that illnesses and injuries that did not come from specific, recognizable causes were believed to be the work of supernatural powers. Therefore, the Egyptians believed, these mysterious ailments could be cured only with magic.

Egyptian Medical Books

The study of Egyptian medicine and all of the magical spells that came with it took dedicated effort, and Egyptian physicians underwent rigorous training. First, they trained as scribes so that they could read the medical texts. Then they were apprenticed to a respected doctor, who was usually part of a temple staff. Since most people went to the gods to ask for healing, physicians practiced in conjunction with the temples. One goddess, Sekhmet, was especially revered for her power to heal and to control epidemics.

Historians know a great deal about Egyptian medical knowledge from a series of New Kingdom medical texts that survive today. These books were used by Egyptian physicians as guides for treating ailments, and they are very different from one another. Some are simply collections and lists of recipes. Others include specific medical treatments for common ailments without the use of magic.

One of these New Kingdom texts, called the *Ebers Papyrus*, stands as one of the most complete and most insightful medical texts to survive from the Egyptian civilization. This extraordinary artifact was clearly the work of a serious, meticulous physician who recorded not only his knowledge but also medical knowledge that had been passed down for countless generations. The *Ebers Papyrus* is a collection of ingredients, recipes, and magical incantations that were collected from more than forty other sources and put together in one encyclopedic work. Most of the writing includes prescriptions for a variety of ailments, specifying the drugs to be used, how much of each drug, and the magical spells that needed to be recited as the drugs were administered.

A statue of the goddess Sekhmet, who Egyptians believed could heal and control epidemics.

Unable to Adapt

Unfortunately, little remains of the knowledge that most Egyptian physicians had. As time went on, physicians' ideas and practices became stagnant. This was mainly due to the Egyptians' persistent inability to apply one kind of knowledge to different types of problems. For example, for centuries Egyptians had practiced mummification on the dead. Through this religious and spiritual process, they gained much practical knowledge about the human body, such as the position of organs and the importance of the heart. But few Egyptians thought to apply it to the study of medicine.

Their efforts were not in vain, however. Although the Egyptians did not seem able to benefit from their own advances in medicine, others did. In later times, the Greeks and the Arabs used the information about anatomy and physiology from Egyptian mummification practices to develop their own medical skills.

Medical knowledge was not the only thing that developed as the New Kingdom progressed. Art, culture, religion, and the power of the king continued to increase until they finally coalesced into one of the richest, most glorious times in Egyptian history: the Eighteenth Dynasty.

The Majesty and Power of the Eighteenth Dynasty

Of all of the periods of New Kingdom history, none glows with the brilliance of the Eighteenth Dynasty. This dynasty was the first one to usher in the New Kingdom era, which began about 1570 B.C., and it is still considered by some to be the greatest age of Egyptian culture. As the Egyptian kings regained power, there was a renewed excitement. Historian George Stendorff describes this unparalleled time in Egyptian civilization:

> In artistic ideals; in the amazing skill of their technical execution; in culture, even to the details of costume and ornament; in social as well as official life, standards are set that were never again attained. All the achievements of Egyptian genius in the thousand years since the building of the pyramids are embodied in this period.[70]

During the Eighteenth Dynasty, trade and conquest brought great wealth to Egypt. Foreign slaves mined the quarries, plowed the fields, and manned the construction sites. Egyptians who had once toiled in these lower-class jobs instead found themselves enjoying the country's new wealth. For the first time, common laborers had the time and money to live a life of comfort and enjoyment.

Public buildings also displayed this wealth and sophistication. Massive palaces and temples were built with seemingly unlimited government funds that came from the foreign invasions. Even ordinary homes displayed a newfound extravagance. Plain household furnishings were replaced with ornate objects, and almost everyone could afford small luxuries such as mirrors, jewelry, and fine clothing.

Artistic achievement reached new heights during this time. Paintings burst with color and life. Sculpture—especially royal statuary—was splendidly carved and showed a new appreciation for a realistic depiction of the human form. Immense temples filled with paintings, carvings, and tomb reliefs filled the cities of Egypt. People could gape in awe at the stunning works and see that, clearly, Egypt was indeed the most powerful place in the world.

The Changing Role of the King

The Eighteenth Dynasty also brought about a revolution in the idea of the king as god. For much of Egyptian history, the king had been considered all-powerful and all-knowing. He alone controlled the lives of his subjects and the lands upon which they lived. As the New Kingdom began, however, this idea changed.

The king continued to live a life apart from the rest of the world, and he was still honored as a god symbolically, but his divinity was clearly less certain than it had been in times past. The King became a more traditional monarch, superior to the commoners but not necessarily as great as the gods. Historian Michael Rice says, "Egypt now entered a phase of its history . . . with the all-powerful ruler surrounded less by reverential awe than by the deference to which absolute power, absolutely manifested, gives occasion."[71]

It is unclear how or why this shift in attitude occurred. Many historians suggest that the years of Hyksos rule shattered any illusions that the Egyptians had of an all-powerful Egyptian king-god who would care for them. They saw for themselves how human—and weak—their rulers could be. Others speculate that the years of bloody warfare had revealed the mortality of Egypt's leaders, and no amount of prayer could bring back the old ideas.

This relief of the pharaoh Seti I as the god Osiris reflects the common belief that the king and the gods were interchangeable.

It was also clear that the king, one man, could no longer—even symbolically—control all of Egypt. The Egyptian society grew to the bursting point during the Eighteenth Dynasty, so much so that the king could no longer single-handedly control the government. Rather than being the all-powerful, godlike ruler of the civilization, the king became merely a strong political leader. According to one historian,

> The administration itself, always one of the most highly developed aspects of Egyptian life, became even more pervasive, a massive bureaucracy usually organized under two powerful viziers, with parallel organizations for each of the Two Kingdoms and an administration which increasingly affected the lives of all the people. The temples developed their own religious bureaucracies still further and exercised a far from benign influence on the political economy.[72]

Regardless of the problems within the Egyptian government during the Eighteenth Dynasty, the kings and queens of the time ruled with a powerful hand, and they brought untold riches into Egypt. Gradually, however, continued warfare and invasion took its toll. By the end of the New Kingdom, a series of

QUEEN HATSHEPSUT

At the beginning of the Eighteenth Dynasty, and of the New Kingdom, Egypt was ruled by many powerful queens. These women, although now much less known than their male counterparts, ushered in the New Kingdom era of luxury and wealth that had never before been seen in Egypt.

The best-known Egyptian queen of the Eighteenth Dynasty was Queen Hatshepsut, who reigned from 1503–1482 B.C. Hatshepsut was a strong, willful woman who desired to rule Egypt in her own name. She was the wife of King Thutmose II, and when he died, his only son (by a royal mistress), Thutmose III, was not yet old enough to rule Egypt. Hatshepsut immediately claimed the throne and soon became supreme ruler.

A hint of her strength of character and ambition comes in the fact that she insisted that she be portrayed in statuary and paintings with the symbolic beard of the Egyptian ruler, even though she was a woman. Most of the surviving statuary of her shows her with the masculine trappings of the kingship.

Like the other Eighteenth Dynasty rulers, Hatshepsut was a prodigious builder. She rebuilt the temples that had been damaged or destroyed in previous years, and her own tomb showed the magnificence of the architecture during her time. It was an enormous structure, with sculptured terraces and delicate architecture.

When Thutmose III became an adult, however, he wanted the throne for himself. He seized the throne from Hatshepsut, then set about destroying all evidence of her rule. He destroyed temples, defaced statuary, and effectively obliterated her name from history. He was so thorough that little evidence remains of her accomplishments. But for the two decades of her rule, her strength and power enabled Egypt to recapture some of its past glory.

weak kings again threw Egypt into turmoil. Priests, seeing the vulnerability of the Egyptian throne, wielded more power in a desperate attempt to maintain control. These events unfolded slowly, over generations. The common Egyptians had no idea that anything was wrong with their world. To them, life continued as it always had. Or so it appeared.

Chapter Six

The Downfall of Egypt

Although the New Kingdom was a glorious time of achievement, it was also the last golden gasp of a great civilization beginning its descent. However, a civilization as enormous and powerful as that of ancient Egypt could not fall overnight. Indeed, it took hundreds of years for the empire to crumble because Egypt's doom did not lie in a single war or other cataclysmic event. Rather, three occurrences—the rise of religions and priests to power, the death of a great Egyptian king, and foreign invasion—drove the grand civilization slowly, but purposefully, to its end.

Religious Strife Weakens Egypt from Within

The first real threat to the civilization came not as an outside enemy but as an Egyptian king. At the end of the Eighteenth Dynasty, the height of Egyptian strength, King Akhenaten rose to the throne in 1379 B.C. The Egyptian people expected that he would be just another strong ruler in a long, stable line of kings before him. However, almost immediately Akhenaten threw Egypt into crisis by rejecting the powerful Egyptian gods and following a single deity. This act created an enormous sense of instability in Egypt because, for the first time, a king had radically altered the way that religion and gods were perceived.

For more than a thousand years, the god Re-Harakhte, also known as Aten, had been the supreme god of Egyptian religion. Most Egyptians believed that he was the great god of all power, and they worshiped him accordingly. At the beginning of the New Kingdom, the city of Thebes (modern-day Karnak) became the Egyptian capital, and with this change of capital cities came a change in the gods. It was normal in Egyptian society for gods to rise and fall in popularity, depending on the personal preferences of the king and the influence of the local gods in powerful cities. As Thebes became more prominent in Egyptian government and politics, the main god of that city, Amen, merged with Re to create Amen Re. Amen Re was believed to be the creator of the world, the victor over enemies, and the controller of life. Soon many people turned their prayers to Amen Re, and the temples and priests who cared for that god rose in prominence.

When Akhenaten came to the throne, he rejected Amen and the idea of worshiping multiple gods outright—a practice that had been established for thousands of years. Even more unusual, he established a new kind of god. He called this god the Aten, but it was strangely different from the old god. This god had no distinctive humanlike image associated with it. Instead, it was depicted as a ray of light flowing from a sun disk. Historian Christine Hobson describes this image:

> This god he now ordered depicted as an image of the sun with rays radiating from it, terminating in hands holding the hieroglyphic symbols for life and power, with himself, his wife and two daughters receiving benefit. This image is frequently described as being the "sun-disk," yet the inscriptions make it clear that the Aten was regarded by the king as being the creative force of the universe that was manifested by the sun. The god himself had no image.[73]

Akhenaten was the first Egyptian to openly worship one god, which was completely unheard of in Egypt. Not only did he change Egyptian religious beliefs, but he also declared that Thebes was no longer Egypt's capital. Instead, he created a new capital city, called Tell el-'Amarna, devoted to Aten worship. He proclaimed that Aten was the supreme ruler and must be worshiped by all Egyptians.

A Single State Religion

At first Akhenaten allowed the temples of the old gods to continue, and most ordinary Egyptians could still worship their traditional gods. However, after a few years Akhenaten closed the temples and declared that Aten worship would be the official state religion. Statuary and paintings depicting other gods and goddesses were destroyed. Nobles and officials who embraced the new beliefs were rewarded. Priests who had followed other gods were outraged.

In the book *The Egyptian Kingdoms*, historian A. Rosalie David explains the changes that Akhenaten wrought in Egypt: "With his queen, Nefertiti, he founded a new capital where he could pursue his worship of the strange, featureless god, Aten. After some years his religion became exclusive and the monuments of other deities were destroyed and defaced, and their priesthoods and worships terminated."[74]

By turning his back on the ancient Egyptian beliefs, Akhenaten single-handedly changed the scope of Egyptian religion. The gods that Egyptians had relied on for centuries suddenly ceased to be important. Deeply held beliefs of the structure of the heavens and the comforting power of the gods to control the world were thrown into uncertainty. Akhenaten forced the Egyptian people to question, and to discard, much of what they held sacred. In doing

In this limestone painting, Queen Nefertiti, Akhenaten, and their daughters worship the god Aten, depicted as a ray of light emanating from a sun disk.

THE ART OF A HERETIC: KING AKHENATEN

Egyptian art had, for centuries, achieved a high level of skill and beauty. But most Egyptian art was stylistically static. Figures were painted the same way they had been for thousands of years.

However, one king sought to change that. King Akhenaten, the heretic king of the New Kingdom, rebelled against the worship of many gods and proclaimed himself—and all of Egyptian society—the follower of only one god. To express his ideas, he initiated a new style of art that strove to portray people in more realistic ways and stressed secular themes.

Considered the heretic king of the New Kingdom, King Akhenaten (whose statue is shown here) promoted new religious and artistic views.

In his book *Egyptian Art*, Egyptian expert Cyril Aldred discusses Akhenaten's influence.

"[Akhenaten] banished at a blow to nearly all the traditional subjects that had been reserved for the decoration of temples since earliest times. . . . Thus, the scene of the pharaoh freeing Egypt from evil forces by dispatching the traditional foes before the god of the temple, was changed to place the slaughtering under the . . . new sun-god, in the presence of the queen and the eldest daughter."

There was also a new element of reality to the statuary and paintings of Akhenaten. Portrait statues show Akhenaten with an elongated face and pronounced chin, suggesting that he had commanded the royal artisans to portray him in a more realistic fashion. Sculptures of the female form show large hips, round buttocks, and protruding stomachs, a vast departure from the slim, idealized figures that were normally created.

so, he sent the society into a crisis of faith and trust from which it never fully recovered.

In addition, he was so obsessed with his new religion that he ignored the growing strife both within the kingdom and outside its borders. He disregarded the growing threat of invaders who conquered Egypt's neighbors and threatened to attack Egypt itself. Letters from the leaders of Egyptian cities, begging for help, went unnoticed. As a result, Egypt declined in military strength and became an open target for conquest.

Struggling to Regroup

Akhenaten's reign lasted only about ten years. When he died, Egypt quickly reverted back to its old beliefs. But the damage had been done. The ousted priests now clung desperately to their gods and their way of life. As historian Michael Rice explains, "After the restoration of the Amen cult and the re-establishment of Thebes as the capital of Egypt the priests were determined to protect and augment their power, and by doing so, to eliminate the risk of another persecution by a heretic or uncompliant king."[75]

More and more, the priests of individual gods fought against one another for power and wealth. No longer would they simply obey the will of a king, and no longer would they allow the king to be the supreme priest of the land. Akhenaten showed the priests that they could no longer trust the throne, and slowly the very foundations of Egyptian religion cracked.

The years following Akhenaten's reign were full of unrest and warfare. Finally, Seti I (reigned 1318–1304 B.C.), the son of Ramses I, managed to defeat these foreign invaders and reestablish some stability to Egypt. According to historian David,

> Sethos [Seti], who with his son was to carry out a policy of restoring former glory, now set out to reconquer Egypt's lost Asiatic empire. . . . The Empire had probably not been abandoned at the end of the Eighteenth Dynasty, but the loyal states were menaced by an increased number of Egypt's enemies. . . . Sethos won the day and restored Egyptian control over part of Syria.[76]

Seti's actions were the last beginning for ancient Egypt. In restoring some of the nation's power, he set the stage for his son, Ramses II, to become one of the most famous, and most respected, Egyptian kings of the New Kingdom.

Ramses II: The Last Great Egyptian King

In Ramses II's youth, he and his father, King Seti, were strong warriors who led many Egyptian campaigns to invade and conquer foreign lands. When Ramses II ascended the throne in 1304 B.C., he was a proud and powerful commander. He was also a very charismatic and commanding man. Because his grandfather, Ramses I, had been a commoner, Ramses II had to prove to the people that he had the right to rule Egypt. He, however, was completely convinced of his right to the throne, and he ruled with unbounded energy and strength.

The Egyptian people seemed to feel that Ramses II was the rightful king, and a poem, written nine years after his coronation, hints at the confidence that Egyptians had in their new, powerful king. It says he was "a champion without his peer, with strong arms and stout heart, beautiful of form like Atum, victorious in all lands. None can take up arms against him; he is a wall for his soldiers, and their shield in the days of battle."[77]

Ramses II left more statuary and buildings than almost any other Egyptian monarch in history, which indicates both his popularity and his complete faith in his own divinity. Historian Cyril Aldred says,

> The monuments of . . . Ramses II abound, a great many having been produced during his long reign of sixty-seven years, in all sizes and materials, and in different styles and qualities. The king proved to be the most industrious builder to occupy the throne of Egypt. Not only were great new constructions raised at Thebes, Memphis, Hermopolis and other large towns in Egypt and in Nubia, but many of the temples still standing desecrated since the days of Akhenaten were rebuilt and reconsecrated in the name of Ramses II.[78]

This forecourt of the Luxor Temple was built to honor King Ramses II.

Ramses II was also known for his successful military campaigns, which solidified his power. He secured Egypt's role in the world by subjugating neighboring countries, then marrying royal princesses from those countries. In this way, he created strong alliances with foreigners that ensured a steady flow of wealth into Egypt. He used this wealth to build the great statues and buildings that are the hallmark of his reign.

Ramses II's prowess in battle gave the Egyptians renewed hope for their land. One song, inscribed on the famous temple of Abu Simbel in Nubia, praises the king for his victories against his enemies. It reveals something about his popularity and his power. The song begins,

> The good god, the strong one, whom men praise, the lord, in whom men make their boast; who protects his soldiers, who makes his boundaries on earth as he will, like Re when he shines over the circle of the world—he the king of Upper and Lower Egypt . . . Ramesses-Beloved-of Amun, who is given life.
>
> He who brings the rebellious ones as captive to Timuris, and the princes with their gifts to his palace. The fear of him courses through their bodies, their limbs tremble in the time of his terribleness. . . . He who sends his arrows against them and has mastery over their limbs . . . the strong lion with claws, loud roaring, sending forth his voice in the valley . . . he, King Ramesses.[79]

By the time of Ramses II's death it seemed that Egypt was once again the most powerful civilization in the universe. The common Egyptian enjoyed a comfortable lifestyle, and the cities were filled with beautiful temples and structures that glorified the gods and the land. There were problems, however. Ramses II left a large number of sons behind, and each one coveted the throne of Egypt. Historians do not completely understand the details of this unrest, but they are certain that, for the next few years, the heirs fought over the right to rule. Most of their reigns were brief, suggesting that the internal political struggle was taking a toll on the government.

As the New Kingdom era came to an end, political corruption touched all parts of the government. A series of bad harvests and famine led many people to rob the rich royal tombs. Warring factions within the government sought to destroy one another, and the priests were only interested in their own quests for power. Ancient Egypt was ripe for its final downfall.

Conquerors Transform Ancient Egypt

With Ramses II's death, Egypt entered a decline from which it would never recover. Because of Egypt's internal turmoil and the rise in power of foreign countries, Egyptian nobles and warriors sought alliances with outsiders for political and financial gain. Ramses II himself had made an alliance with the Hittites, a powerful foreign regime of the time. Other countries also rose to power and began a series of invasions. The Libyans took advantage of the chaos in Egypt and took power of the Egyptian throne in about 945 B.C. Furthermore, leaders from other countries, such as Judah and Israel, controlled some areas of Egypt.

In 770 B.C. Kushites from Nubia, under the command of their ruler, Piankhi, surrounded and easily conquered Egypt. Eventually Kushites controlled the Egyptian throne, and although they continued to worship the Egyptian gods and build temples and tombs, the true Egyptian civilization had already begun to disappear. These kings had a great sense of religious purpose and an honest, deep love of the Egypt of the past. They believed it was their destiny to revive the old ways and to reestablish some of the gods and the glory of Egypt. They ruled Egypt for more than a hundred years, and many Egyptians welcomed them. As Aldred contends,

> They [the Kushites] were welcomed in Upper Egypt, and secured, by force of arms where necessary, the loyalty of Lower Egyptian princes and their vassals. They brought order and stability to a divided realm. A deep veneration for tradition was inherent in their outlook, and research was undertaken into ancient and sacred literature.[80]

In 525 B.C. Egypt became part of the Persian Empire. Although the Persians seemed to have some respect for Egyptian culture and society, they saw the country simply as part of their vast empire. For the next two hundred years, Egyptian kings struggled unsuccessfully to regain control from the Persians. The Persian kings held the Egyptians tightly, and the country ultimately became another Persian province.

But the destruction of Persia was on the horizon. In 332 B.C. Macedonian king Alexander the Great reached Egypt, and the Persians surrendered Egypt to him without a fight. He appointed native governors, left an

KING TUT'S TOMB

The single most famous Egyptian tomb is that of King Tutankhamen, a ruler who came to the throne after King Akhenaten as a boy of only nine. Images of King Tut's magnificent golden mask have become synonymous with the idea of Egyptian kings. What few people know is that King Tutankhamen was a minor king who died when he was still a teenager, the son of the infamous King Akhenaten and one of his minor wives, Queen Kiya.

Furthermore, it was an ancient accident that preserved his tomb at all. Most of the tombs in the Valley of the Kings, where King Tut was buried, had been ransacked centuries before King Tut's discovery. However, in about 1140 B.C., laborers working on the great tomb of Ramses VI unintentionally piled rocks over the entrance of a tiny, forgotten tomb. This construction debris effectively hid King Tut from tomb robbers and the rest of the world for three thousand years.

During the 1920s a promising archaeologist named Howard Carter partnered with a wealthy Englishman named Lord Carnarvon, and together they explored the Valley of the Kings for ten years. On the morning of November 4, 1922, Carter arrived at the work site and immediately knew that something exciting had happened. Workers had uncovered sixteen steps leading downward. At the bottom, a walled-up entrance included unbroken seals of a little-known king named Tutankhamen. When all the rubble was cleared, Carter slowly opened the door. Carter later described his discovery in Christine Hobson's book *The World of the Pharoahs*,

"With trembling hands I made a tiny breach in the upper left hand corner. . . . Candle tests were applied as a precaution against foul gases and then, widening the hole a little, I inserted the candle and peered in. At first I could see nothing, the hot air escaping from the chamber causing the candle flame to flicker but presently, as my eyes grew accustomed to the light, details of the room within emerged slowly from the mist; strange animals, statues and gold—everywhere the glint of gold. For the moment I was struck dumb with amazement, and when Lord Carnarvon, unable to stand the suspense any longer, inquired anxiously, 'Can you see anything?' it was all I could do to get [out] the words, 'Yes, wonderful things!'"

It took Carter and a team of workers more than ten years to remove and catalog all of the treasures of the tomb. There was such a huge quantity of materials and objects that Carter himself never completed his study of them. He died in 1939, and to this day there has not been a complete study of the treasures of King Tut.

army in Egypt under the general Ptolemy, founded the city of Alexandria, and then left Egypt.

The Ptolemies

When Alexander the Great died a few years later, his vast kingdom was divided among his generals, and Ptolemy took control of Egypt. For the next few centuries, a line of fifteen Ptolemies ruled the country.

The time of the Ptolemaic rule was one of great despair for native Egyptians. According to historian David,

> The Ptolemaic period was a time of great intellectual achievement in Egypt, yet also one of severe deprivation and humiliation for the native Egyptians. On the one hand, the Ptolemies created the beautiful city of Alexandria on the shores of the Mediterranean which became an intellectual center, attracting the most eminent scholars of the ancient world. . . . On the other hand, the Ptolemies, by using to their own advantage the divine power of the pharaoh, brutally exploited the land and the native inhabitants of Egypt.[81]

One example of this is in the way that the Ptolemaic kings controlled agriculture in the still-rich Nile valley. Although the king had symbolically owned the land for centuries, in practice, that law had never been enforced. The Ptolemies, however, seized ownership of everything in the name of the king. People could no longer own private land, and the government regulated what crops could be grown. The Ptolemies used the divine power of the king as god against the Egyptians, forcing landowners to become tenants on their own land.

The Ptolemies also encouraged people from other lands to immigrate to Egypt, and soon many high government posts were held by Greeks, Persians, and others. Greeks served in the army and became the artisans of the state. Gradually, Egyptians became foreigners in their own country. One historian explains,

> Ptolemy offered the Greeks the opportunity of high government posts and gifts of land. They, and not the Egyptians, served in the army and navy and flourished as traders and artisans. The Ptolemies showed marked favor to their non-Egyptian subjects, who repaid them with loyalty. In predominately Greek cities, such as Alexandria and Naukratis, the Egyptians were considered as "foreigners," and throughout the land two distinct communities existed—the downtrodden natives and the favored foreigners.[82]

These outsiders brought their own languages, cultures, beliefs, and traditions with them to Egypt. As they rose in power and influence, so did their ways of life. Slowly, Egyptian ways of life, their language, and their entire culture were replaced and forgotten.

Cleopatra and the Romans

By 69 B.C., the Ptolemies' strength was failing. The Romans were rising in power and influence, so the Ptolemies created an alliance with them. Instead of ensuring safety, however, this alliance only made the Romans seek control over Egypt. The Ptolemies had to pay tributes in the form of gold, slaves, and goods to keep the Romans away from Egypt.

Cleopatra was the daughter of Ptolemy XII. When she was seventeen her father died, and she became joint ruler of Egypt along with her eleven-year-old brother, Ptolemy XIII, on the condition that she marry him. The two did marry, but Cleopatra soon dropped his name from any official documents and had her own portrait and name printed on coins of that time. Historians speculate that this was Cleopatra's attempt to become the sole ruler of Egypt, but it backfired. Three years later, in 49 B.C., Ptolemy XIII listened to his advisers and drove Cleopatra into exile. While she was in exile, Cleopatra gathered an army to fight her brother for the throne. She also turned to the hated Romans and gained a powerful ally—Julius Caesar.

During that time, the Romans achieved power within the Egyptian government by supporting different political factions that rose to prominence with their help. Although the Romans worked behind the scenes, they wielded a great deal of power in Egypt. Cleopatra sought the alliance with Caesar to solidify her own power within the government, and the two became lovers as well as political partners.

In 47 B.C. Cleopatra and Caesar returned to Egypt to defeat Ptolemy's army and kill her brother. Caesar was successful, and this victory led him to become one of the most famous and powerful military leaders of the age. However, many of his political foes despised his actions and condemned him for his relationship with Cleopatra, an enemy queen.

Although the Romans were on the verge of completely controlling Egypt, Caesar declared Cleopatra queen—infuriating his Roman enemies and causing a great scandal in Rome. His loyalty to Cleopatra was considered to be treason, and his enemies began to rise against him. In 44 B.C. Caesar was assassinated by his senators, powerful Roman politicians, who felt he had been a traitor to Rome.

Following Caesar's murder, Rome split between two other powerful Romans: Mark Antony and Octavian (later to become the Roman emperor Caesar Augustus). Antony, who married Octavian's sister, summoned Cleopatra to Rome and almost immediately fell in love with her. His love blinded him to the growing political unrest and danger from his rival, Octavian. Antony returned to Egypt to be with Cleopatra, but Octavian, and Rome, were furious. The Roman senators denounced Cleopatra as a sorceress. Finally, Octavian declared war on Cleopatra and Mark Antony in 32 B.C.

The last ruler of Egypt, Queen Cleopatra waged war against her brother for the throne but was unable to prevent Rome from defeating her empire.

THE REAL CLEOPATRA

The name *Cleopatra* is synonymous with love, sex, betrayal, and suicide. She is one of the most glamorous figures in Egyptian history. But few know that she was actually a very good ruler who was loved by the Egyptian people. Her reputation as a seductress overshadowed her political and personal accomplishments, and her vilification by the Romans upon her death sealed her undeserved infamy in history.

Cleopatra was raised in the royal household, and she was well educated as a child. Not only was she a quick student, but she also became fluent in nine languages, was a mathematician, and was a shrewd businesswoman. In later years ambassadors and foreigners marveled at her command of languages and at her astounding intellect, for she could converse with them intelligently on a variety of subjects, including politics, warfare, medicine, and religion.

Although Cleopatra was a Ptolemaic ruler, she considered herself Egyptian. She was the only Ptolemaic ruler to speak the Egyptian language, and this endeared her to her subjects in a way that nothing else did. During the time of her rule, the world was enveloped in war, so there is little information about the kind of ruler Cleopatra was. Scarce evidence of her reign survives, but it is clear from texts and other sources that she was a beloved queen. She was devoted to Egypt, and scholars believe her actions were an attempt to keep her country together and away from Roman hands. At the time, Rome had a stranglehold on Egypt, and Cleopatra recognized the threat the empire posed to her beloved world. She was smart enough to realize that an alliance with Rome might benefit her country, and she sought that alliance in the best way she knew how.

Off the coast of Greece the two armies met at Actium, one of the most famous sea battles in history. During the battle, Cleopatra—convinced that Antony would be defeated—withdrew her forces and forced Antony to surrender. They fled together to the city of Alexandria, and as Octavian marched to the city, they commited suicide rather than being taken prisoner.

With Cleopatra's death, her kingdom became a province of the Roman Empire. Egypt was still a rich, profitable area, and the Romans took great pains to maintain it. However, the yields of Egypt's vast farmlands were now shipped to Rome, and Egypt slowly became little more than a commodity for the powerful Roman Empire. The great ancient Egyptian civilization had ended.

EPILOGUE

Rediscovering Egypt's Past

For centuries, ancient Egypt remained a mystery. In the classical times of ancient Greece, travelers such as the historian Herodotus sought to discover the ancient Egyptian civilization, with little success. Roman emperors began plundering Egypt for its artworks and its gold, and by the sixteenth century, European merchants were taking Egyptian objects by the wagonload back to their homelands. There was a huge market for these unusual objects, and people were willing to pay high prices for a piece of the mysterious Egyptian past.

Napoléon's Fascination with Egypt

By the nineteenth century, the desire for Egyptian artifacts had reached a peak. Travelers from around the world braved the heat and the desert to see the once-great Egyptian cities and collect as many objects as they could find. This obsession for all things Egyptian grew to dizzying heights as a result of Napoléon Bonaparte's military campaign into Egypt in 1799. This military action introduced the world to the glory of ancient Egypt, and scientists and scholars around the world became fascinated with the mysterious ancient Egyptians. They sought to learn more about the civilization through research and study rather than plunder and destruction. This ushered in the golden age of Egyptian archaeology.

Napoléon himself was fascinated with Egypt's past. Even as he conquered Egypt and organized the government, he also set up archaeological expeditions and scientific studies of the ruins of Egypt. According to one writer,

> the focus was, above all, on Egypt's past. . . . The archaeological expeditions at ancient Thebes, modern Luxor and Karnak, the discovery of the Rosetta Stone, and the drawings done by Vivant Denon's team for the *Description of Egypt* [a nineteenth-century book about the country] all demonstrate the lively curiosity felt even by simple soldiers for that lost world.[83]

The *Description of Egypt* was an encyclopedic volume that detailed every aspect of Egypt. Napoléon had the book printed on his orders, and it contained more than three thousand illustrations, including detailed drawings of the ruins of buildings, temples, and tombs.

Napoléon's campaign and the publication of the *Description of Egypt* ignited imaginations around the world. Egypt became fashionable in Europe, and suddenly everyone wanted to visit Egypt and dig for treasures. At first, the visitors came and plundered whatever treasures they could find. There were no laws against looting, and most of the treasures were taken legally. Excavators by the hundreds descended on Egypt, digging up countless artifacts and selling them to museums all over the world.

Alarmed by the growing numbers of objects being taken from Egypt, the country's government began passing laws against wholesale thievery. By the end of the nineteenth century, most of the widespread looting had been replaced with organized and sanctioned scholarly digs.

Early Egyptologists

Some of the first explorers were artists and scholars fascinated with the Egyptian hieroglyphs. Englishman John Gardner Wilkinson was born in 1797. One of his school teachers, George Butler, was so enthusiastic about Egyptology that the young Wilkinson became passionate about the subject as well. At the time, very little real scholarship had ever been done on Egyptian ruins, so Wilkinson set out to study as much as he could. He eventually lived in Egypt for twelve years, from 1821 to 1833, sketching everything he

After conquering Egypt in 1799, Napoléon Bonaparte set up archaeological expeditions and scientific studies of the Egyptian ruins.

saw. He took it upon himself to learn to speak Arabic and to read and write Coptic, which many thought was a later form of ancient Egyptian and the key to unlocking the language of the hieroglyphs.

Although he never translated the hieroglyphs himself, his work laid the foundation for Jean-François Champollion's translation some years later. Wilkinson's work was so respected that, as Christine Hobson relates, "His scholarship was acclaimed everywhere and, in 1839, he received a knighthood from the hands of the young Queen Victoria of England, the only Egyptologist ever honored in such a fashion for his work."[84]

Few Egyptologists contributed so much to the understanding of the ancient Egyptians as Wilkinson did. He covered more than fifty subjects, including hieroglyphs, customs, daily life, and astronomy. Although he studied ancient Egypt with what are now considered primitive materials, many of his discoveries and ideas about ancient Egyptian life remain to this day.

Jean-François Champollion deciphered the Egyptian hieroglyphs in 1822.

Amelia Edwards and the Egypt Exploration Fund

Amelia Edwards was a colorful, intelligent woman who thrived on adventure. She published a novel when she was in her twenties, and the income from it enabled her to travel throughout Egypt. She explored Egypt as a tourist, staying in hotels and flourishing on the excitement of a crocodile hunt. But her writer's eye and her love of Egyptian history soon turned to more dismal subjects.

During a trip to Egypt in 1873 Edwards was dismayed at the way tourists spoiled and vandalized many of the Egyptian monuments. She was only in Egypt for three months, but the trip changed her life. Not one to stand idly by, she returned to England and began writing letters to all of the eminent Egyptologists of the day, asking them for help in starting a fund for legitimate study of Egyptian antiquities. Her efforts resulted in the formation of the Egypt Exploration Fund at the British Museum.

The fund, established to help honest excavators and explorers do their work, financed numerous excavations at Egyptian sites over the course of many years. Today, it continues to fund scientists and scholars who study the ancient Egyptian civilization.

A Child Prodigy Breaks the Hieroglyph Code

Almost a hundred years before Edwards formed the Egypt Exploration fund, Jean-François Champollion was born. At that time, 1799, Napoléon's accounts of the wonders of the ancient civilization were beginning to spread throughout Europe. As a small boy, Champollion vowed to be the first person to unlock the secrets of the hieroglyphs, and he set out to arm himself with all of the knowledge he would need to do so.

While he was a student at the University of Grenoble in France, he diligently studied Hebrew, Arabic, Syriac, and Aramaic languages as well as Latin and Greek. By the time he was seventeen, he was studying the ancient Coptic language. Two years later, he became a professor of ancient history at his old school, Grenoble.

For years Champollion studied the mysterious hieroglyph symbols and the writings of scholars who came before him. At the time, all scholars struggled with the same question: Were the symbols phonetic, each representing a sound? Or did each symbol represent a separate idea? Without the answer to this puzzle, Champollion knew that the secrets of ancient Egypt would not be brought to light.

He sought the answer to those questions by studying the Rosetta Stone. First, Champollion discovered that every ruler's name was enclosed within an oval, called a cartouche. Some of the cartouches had already been translated by others, and he could distinguish the names of Ptolemy and Cleopatra within the text.

After he had established the meanings of these few symbols, Champollion realized that the hieroglyphs were a combination of symbols that represented both ideas and phonetic sounds. Only certain signs were intended to be read as words. The others represented concepts, such as god or king. The Egyptians combined word hieroglyphs and concept hieroglyphs to create their language.

On September 27, 1822, Champollion announced his discovery. Immediately, other scholars seized his ideas and began their own deciphering. The riddle of the hieroglyphs had been solved.

The Legacy of Ancient Egypt

From the moment that Champollion unlocked the code of the hieroglyphs, it became increasingly clear that no ancient civilization had a greater impact on the world than that of the ancient Egyptians. Their culture, religion, and society dominated the world for countless generations. Even today, their legacy can be felt in almost every part of human existence.

The grand Egyptian pyramids of the Old Kingdom continue to inspire the builders of the world. The simple, elegant pyramid design is timeless, and architects around the world have emulated its awe-inspiring effect in a variety of ways. In Paris, France, for example, a huge glass pyramid stands at the entrance of the Louvre museum. And in Memphis, Tennessee, a huge pyramid sits beside the Mississippi River as a tourist attraction and visitor's center.

Egyptian medicine and science contributed to a greater understanding of the human body and how it worked. The knowledge that the ancient Egyptians had about anatomy and medicine was eventually passed down to the Greeks and Arabs, who became renowned for their medical skills. Their knowledge—based in part on Egyptian learning—became the foundation for medicine today.

Egyptian art still has the ability to influence cultures of the world. Jewelry, furniture, and other objects have been endlessly copied and reproduced, adding to the popular cultures of modern society. Many people

Evidence that ancient Egyptian culture continues to shape the world can be seen in the pyramid-inspired architecture of the entrance to the Louvre Museum in Paris.

still respect and study the ancient Egyptian religions, believing in the gods that once ruled the earth and lived in the mighty temples of the Egyptian kings.

Through plague, floods, war, strife, and political turmoil, the Egyptian civilization continued onward. It was so powerful that, even after centuries of neglect, it rose once again from the golden, dusty ruins to fire the imaginations of countless people. Ancient Egypt still has the power to change the world, and this is a testament to the strength and power of those who built it so very long ago.

NOTES

Chapter 1: Before the Egyptians

1. Michael Hoffman, *Egypt Before the Pharaohs*. New York: Alfred Knopf, 1979, p. 17.
2. Hoffman, *Egypt Before the Pharaohs*, p. xvii.
3. Adoph Erman, *The Literature of the Ancient Egyptians*, New York: Arno, 1977, p. 146.
4. Hoffman, *Egypt Before the Pharaohs*, p. 143.
5. Hoffman, *Egypt Before the Pharaohs*, p. 143.
6. Michael Rice, *Egypt's Making*, London: Routledge, 1990, p. 33.
7. Rice, *Egypt's Making*, p. 170.
8. Rice, *Egypt's Making*, p. 170.
9. Hoffman, *Egypt Before the Pharoahs*, p. 127.
10. Dennis Forbes, "Quibell at Hierakonpolis," *KMT: A Modern Journal of Ancient Egypt*, Fall 1996, vol. 7, no. 3, p. 52.

Chapter 2: The King and His People

11. Stephen Quirke, ed., *The British Museum Book of Ancient Egypt*. London: Thames and Hudson, 1992, p. 69.
12. Quoted in Guillemette Andreu, *Egypt in the Age of the Pyramids*. Ithaca, NY: Cornell University Press, 1997, p. 13.
13. Douglas Brewer and Emily Teeter, *Egypt and the Egyptians*. London: Cambridge University Press, 1999, p. 69.
14. Quoted in Barry Kemp, *Ancient Egypt: Anatomy of a Civilization*. London: Routledge, 1989, pp. 30–31.
15. Kemp, *Ancient Egypt*, p. 37.
16. Quoted in Edward Wente, *Letters from Ancient Egypt*. Atlanta: Scholars, 1990, pp. 18–19.
17. Quoted in Andreu, *Egypt in the Age of the Pyramids*, p. 18.
18. Brewer and Teeter, *Egypt and the Egyptians*, p. 71.
19. Kemp, *Ancient Egypt*, p. 191.
20. Herodotus, *The Histories*, trans. Robin Waterfield. New York: Oxford University Press, 1998, pp. 109–10.
21. Brewer and Teeter, *Egypt and the Egyptians*, p. 77.
22. Brewer and Teeter, *Egypt and the Egyptians*, pp. 77–78.
23. Christine Hobson, *The World of the Pharaohs*. London: Thames and Hudson, 1987, p. 162.

Chapter 3: The Glory of Egypt: The Old Kingdom

24. Michael Rice, *Egypt's Legacy*. New York: Routledge, 1997, p. 101.
25. Hobson, *The World of the Pharaohs*, 1987, p. 64.

26. Rice, *Egypt's Legacy*, p. 102.
27. Rice, *Egypt's Legacy*, p. 103.
28. Hobson, *The World of the Pharaohs*, p. 76.
29. A. Rosalie David, *The Egyptian Kingdoms*. New York: Peter Bedrick Books, 1975, p. 80.
30. Brewer and Teeter, *Egypt and the Egyptians*, p. 84.
31. Brewer and Teeter, *Egypt and the Egyptians*, p. 84.
32. Brewer and Teeter, *Egypt and the Egyptians*, p. 85.
33. Christine El Mahdy, *Mummies: Myth and Magic*. New York: Thames and Hudson, 1989, p. 140.
34. Brewer and Teeter, *Egypt and the Egyptians*, p. 86.
35. Quoted in Brewer and Teeter, *Egypt and the Egyptians*, p. 86.
36. Quoted in Brewer and Teeter, *Egypt and the Egyptians*, p. 147.
37. El Mahdy, *Mummies*, p. 12.
38. James Henry Breasted, *History of Egypt from the Earliest Times to the Persian Conquest*. London: Hodder & Stoughton, 1905, pp. 63–64.
39. Quoted in Brewer and Teeter, *Egypt and the Egyptians*, p. 147.
40. Brewer and Teeter, *Egypt and the Egyptians*, p. 148.
41. Quoted in Wente, *Letters from Ancient Egypt*, p. 100.
42. Quoted in R. B. Parkinson, *Voices from Ancient Egypt*, Norman: University of Oklahoma Press, 1991, p. 133.

Chapter 4: The Flowering of Egypt: The Middle Kingdom

43. Rice, *Egypt's Legacy*, p. 125.
44. Rice, *Egypt's Legacy*, p. 137.
45. Cyril Aldred, *Egyptian Art*. London: Thames and Hudson, 1980, p. 138.
46. Brewer and Teeter, *Egypt and the Egyptians*, p. 18.
47. Rice, *Egypt's Legacy*, pp. 135–36.
48. Hobson, *The World of the Pharaohs*, p. 138.
49. Quoted in Hobson, *The World of the Pharaohs*, p. 89.
50. David, *The Egyptian Kingdoms*, p. 71.
51. Rice, *Egypt's Legacy*, p. 136.
52. Aldred, *Egyptian Art*, pp. 122–23.
53. Rice, *Egypt's Legacy*, p. 138.
54. David, *The Egyptian Kingdoms*, p. 71.
55. Quoted in Leonard Cottrell, *Life Under the Pharaohs*. New York: Holt, Rinehart, and Winston, 1960, p. 162.
56. George Stendorff, *Egypt*. New York: J. J. Augustin, 1943, p. 71.
57. Breasted, *History of Egypt from the Earliest Times to the Persian Conquest*, p. 203.
58. Breasted, *History of Egypt from the Earliest Times to the Persian Conquest*, p. 204.

Chapter 5: The Last Great Age: The New Kingdom

59. Quoted in Breasted, *History of Egypt from the Earliest Times to the Persian Conquest*, p. 216.
60. David, *The Egyptian Kingdoms*, p. 21.
61. Quoted in Stendorff, *Egypt*, p. 89.

62. Aldred, *Egyptian Art*, p. 141.
63. Aldred, *Egyptian Art*, p. 141.
64. Breasted, *History of Egypt from the Earliest Times to the Persian Conquest*, p. 233.
65. David, *The Egyptian Kingdoms*, p. 116.
66. Quoted in Brewer and Teeter, *Egypt and the Egyptians*, p. 74.
67. Quoted in Cottrell, *Life Under the Pharaohs*, p. 114.
68. El Mahdy, *Mummies*, p. 140.
69. David, *The Egyptian Kingdoms*, p. 115.
70. Stendorff, *Egypt*, p. 104.
71. Rice, *Egypt's Legacy*, p. 147.
72. Rice, *Egypt's Legacy*, p. 147.

Chapter 6: The Downfall of Egypt

73. Hobson, *The World of the Pharaohs*, p. 106.
74. David, *The Egyptian Kingdoms*, p. 23.
75. Rice, *Egypt's Legacy*, p. 174.
76. David, *The Egyptian Kingdoms*, p. 26.
77. Quoted in Erman, *The Literature of the Ancient Egyptians*, p. 260.
78. Aldred, *Egyptian Art*, pp. 190–91.
79. Quoted in Erman, *The Literature of the Ancient Egyptians*, p. 259.
80. Aldred, *Egyptian Art*, p. 215.
81. David, *The Egyptian Kingdoms*, p. 31.
82. David, *The Egyptian Kingdoms*, p. 32.

Epilogue: Rediscovering Egypt's Past

83. Quoted in Jean Vercoutter, *The Search for Ancient Egypt*. New York: Harry Abrams, 1992, p. 135.
84. Hobson, *The World of the Pharaohs*, p. 37.

FOR FURTHER READING

George Hart, *Eyewitness Book of Ancient Egypt*. London: Dorling Kindersley, 1990. This children's book is chock-full of interesting information and wonderful photos of objects that made up the daily lives of ordinary Egyptians.

Mark Lehner, *The Complete Pyramids: Solving the Ancient Mysteries*. London: Thames and Hudson, 1997. This fully illustrated book, by one of the premiere Egyptologists of the late twentieth century, includes information about every Egyptian pyramid.

David Silverman, *Ancient Egypt*. London: Oxford University Press, 1997. This lavishly illustrated book includes information from twelve Egyptian scholars. Their essays cover such topics as history, legends, geography, and religion of the Egyptians.

Works Consulted

Books

Cyril Aldred, *Egypt to the End of the Old Kingdom*. London: Thames and Hudson, 1988. A scholarly work that follows the development of the earliest part of the Egyptian civilization.

———, *Egyptian Art*. London: Thames and Hudson, 1980. This work details the various kinds of artwork for which the Egyptians were celebrated, including tomb paintings and sculpture.

Guillemette Andreu, *Egypt in the Age of the Pyramids*. Ithaca, NY: Cornell University Press, 1997. This book is a complete summary of Egyptian civilization, specifically during the time of the construction of the great pyramids.

James Henry Breasted, *History of Egypt from the Earliest Times to the Persian Conquest*. London: Hodder & Stoughton, 1905. This encyclopedia, published at the turn of the twentieth century, is one of the most exhaustive accounts of Egyptian civilization ever published.

Douglas Brewer and Emily Teeter, *Egypt and the Egyptians*. London: Cambridge University Press, 1999. A very readable, detailed explanation of every aspect of Egyptian life, from peasants to rulers.

Leonard Cottrell, *Life Under the Pharaohs*. New York: Holt, Rinehart, and Winston, 1960. A whimsical, part fiction, part fact, account of daily life in Egypt. This book uses primary source materials to imagine what life in Egypt would have been like.

A. Rosalie David, *Discovering Ancient Egypt*. New York: Facts On File, 1993. A detailed listing of all of the archaeological sites in Egypt and a complete history of the Egyptian civilization.

———, *The Egyptian Kingdoms*. New York: Peter Bedrick Books, 1975. This is a well-researched guide to the history of Egyptian exploration and history.

Ikram Dodson, *The Mummy in Ancient Egypt*. London: Thames and Hudson, 1998. This book details the history of the mummy and its meaning to the Egyptians.

Sergio Donadoni, ed., *The Egyptians*. Chicago: University of Chicago Press, 1997. This overview book touches on many Egyptian themes, including art, architecture, and daily life.

Christine El Mahdy, *Mummies: Myth and Magic*. New York: Thames and Hudson, 1989. This is a complete guide to the history of mummy making, from the earliest Egyptian rituals. Modern-day analysis, including X rays of mummies, is also included.

Adolph Erman, *The Literature of the Ancient Egyptians*. New York: Arno, 1977. This is a wonderful, yet somewhat scholarly, translation of Egyptian letters, tomb inscriptions, and religious documents that give a fascinating glimpse into the lives of Egyptians.

Herodotus, *The Histories*. Trans. Robin Waterfield. New York: Oxford University Press, 1998. Herodotus, considered to be one of the world's greatest historians, delivers his account of the history of the world. Book 2 of his book details his travels in Egypt during the time of Greek occupation and explains many of the daily practices of Egyptians that date back centuries.

Christine Hobson, *The World of the Pharaohs*. London: Thames and Hudson, 1987. This book describes the explorers who rediscovered ancient Egypt and details their archaeological discoveries.

Michael Hoffman, *Egypt Before the Pharaohs*. New York: Alfred Knopf, 1979. This exhaustive volume details the history of Egyptian prehistory before the beginning of the Old Kingdom.

Erik Hornug, *The Egyptians*. Chicago: University of Chicago Press, 1990. Every aspect of Egyptian life is explained in this scholarly work.

Barry Kemp, *Ancient Egypt: Anatomy of a Civilization*. London: Routledge, 1989. This work deals mainly with the psychology of the Egyptians and offers theories for their beliefs, the role of the king, and other aspects of Egyptian life.

R. B. Parkinson, *Voices from Ancient Egypt*. Norman: University of Oklahoma Press, 1991. Parkinson has included many delightful first-person writings from Egyptian papyrus texts, including prayers and letters that were written more than three thousand years ago.

William Flinders Petrie, *Wisdom of the Egyptians*. London: British School of Archaeology in Egypt, 1940. The "Father of Egyptology" writes about the science and mathematic aspects of Egyptian life.

Stephen Quirke, ed., *The British Museum Book of Ancient Egypt*. London: Thames and Hudson, 1992. This nicely illustrated book follows the history of the Egyptian civilization.

Michael Rice, *Egypt's Legacy*. New York: Routledge, 1997. This book deals mainly with predynastic Egypt and the Old Kingdom, giving readers an idea of what the earliest Egyptians were like.

———, *Egypt's Making*. New York: Routledge, 1990. Rice digs even further into Egypt's past with this book, highlighting the earliest times in Egypt's long history.

Waley-el-dine Sameh, *Daily Life in Ancient Egypt*. New York: McGraw-Hill, 1964. Sameh details the lives of the Egyptians with lavish photos of artifacts and tomb paintings that detail all aspects of ancient life, from children's games to rituals of the dead.

George Stendorff, *Egypt*. New York: J. J. Augustin, 1943. A scholarly compendium of Egyptian history that focuses on Egyptian archaeology.

G. P. F. Van der Boorn, *The Duties of the Vizier*. New York: Kegan Paul International, 1988. This scholarly treatise details the lives and duties of the royal viziers of Egypt.

Jean Vercoutter, *The Search for Ancient Egypt*. New York: Harry Abrams, 1992. This volume, part of the Discoveries series, focuses mainly on anecdotes and interesting information about the rediscovery of Egypt in the nineteenth century.

Edward Wente, *Letters from Ancient Egypt*. Atlanta: Scholars, 1990. Wente has compiled an amazing array of personal correspondence from the Egyptian civilization, including letters to and from the king, legal documents, and private letters from workers and ordinary Egyptian citizens.

Periodicals

Dennis Forbes, "Quibell at Hierakonpolis," *KMT: A Modern Journal of Ancient Egypt*, Fall 1996.

S. R. K. Glanville, "The Letters of Aahmose of Peniati," *Journal of Egyptian Archaeology*, 1928.

Index

Picture Credits

Cover photo: Archivo Iconografico, S.A./Corbis
Archive Photos, 29, 35, 39, 62, 74, 78
© Archivo Iconografico, S.A./Corbis, 16
© Bojan Brecelj/Corbis, 32, 53
Borromeo/Art Resource, NY, 43, 66
© Charles Walker Collection/Stock Montage, Inc., 42
© Elio Ciol/Corbis, 61
© Corbis, 38
Dover Publications, 41
Giraudon/Art Resource, NY, 72
© Charles & Josette Lenars/Corbis, 55
Eric Lessing/Art Resource, NY, 7, 20, 68
Library of Congress, 37, 52
© Richard List/Corbis, 84
© Michael Nicholson/Corbis, 51
North Wind Picture Archives, 10, 23, 24, 82
© Gianni Dagli Orti/Corbis, 14, 28, 48, 54, 59
Reuters/HO/Archive Photos, 40
Scala/Art Resource, NY, 31, 71
Stock Montage, Inc., 21, 47, 63, 81

About the Author

Award-winning children's magazine editor and writer Allison Lassieur has published more than two dozen books about history, world cultures, current events, science, and health. She has written for magazines such as *National Geographic World*, *Highlights for Children*, *Scholastic News*, and *Disney Adventures*, and she also writes puzzle books and computer-game materials. In addition to writing, Ms. Lassieur studies medieval textile history. She lives and works with her two cats, Ulysses and Oberon, in a one-hundred-year-old house in Easton, Pennsylvania.